ROYAL AIR FORCE
SECOND EDITION

Paul Jackson

IAN ALLAN
Publishing

First published 1992
Completely revised second edition 1995

ISBN 0 7110 2338 7

Published by Ian Allan Publishing

an imprint of Ian Allan Ltd, Terminal
House, Station Approach, Shepperton,
Surrey TW17 8AS.
Printed by Ian Allan Printing Ltd,
Coombelands House, Coombelands Lane,
Addlestone, Weybridge,
Surrey KT15 1HY.

Title page:
RAF on display. The 75th anniversary
celebrations in 1993 were dampened by heav■
rain at Marham but provided an opportunity ■
most jet and helicopter units to present
themselves to HM The Queen. Since that time
the Buccaneers, Jet Provosts and Hunters visi■
have been withdrawn and the Andover E3
transferred to a civilian operator. *Paul Jackso■*

Below:
A grey-camouflaged Jaguar over Bosnia is
representative of the latest peace-keeping
operation to stretch RAF resources. *RAF*

Front cover:
Boeing Helicopters Chinook HC2. *Denis J. Calv■*

Back cover:
Panavia Tornado F3s. *BAe Defence Ltd*

Contents

Addenda	Page	3
Introduction	Page	4
1 Stations	Page	7
2 Flying units	Page	19
3 Aircraft and missiles	Page	41
4 Aircraft identity markings	Page	63
5 The RAF in action	Page	71
6 RAF Regiment, Reserves and Auxiliaries	Page	81
7 Radars for control and defence	Page	87
8 Names, ranks and numbers	Page	94

ADDENDA

Changes in RAF organisation and equipment implemented or announced immediately prior to publication are summarised below.

p10 Cranwell; final Tucano course (No 111) graduated on 7 April and aircraft transferred to Linton and Topcliffe (type officially withdrawn on 31 March). No 3 FTS becomes the parent of aircraft transferring from Finningley. JEFTS Fireflies at Barkston will begin training Army personnel formerly instructed on Chipmunks at Middle Wallop.

p10 Closure date for Finningley (and disbandment for No 6 FTS) is 31 March 1996; Dominies and Jetstreams (Air Navigation School, Air Electronic Engineers' & Loadmasters' School and METS) to Cranwell by September-October 1995; Hawk Squadron (including JFACSTU) to Valley in July 1995; Bulldogs and Tucanos to Topcliffe in May 1995; No 9 AEF and Yorkshire UAS to Church Fenton by September 1995; No 100 Sqn to Leeming by October 1995. Two Jetstreams may be converted for transport duties.

p14 Closure date for Scampton is 31 March 1996; Bulldogs to Cranwell in March 1995, CFS HQ following in May; Tucanos to Topcliffe in April 1995; Red Arrows to Marham in September 1995; Trade Management Training School to Cosford, date undecided; JACIG (which formed on 1 July 1990) and its Andover to re-locate; Rapier Caderisation Unit to Waddington.

p16 Newton lost its autonomy on 31 March 1995 and is now an out-station of Cranwell. Training Development and Support Unit to Halton on 10 March 1995.

p17 Swanton Morley's closure date is 6 September 1995.

p25 No 27 Sqn has adopted the code range NA-NZ (assigned backwards) for its Chinooks.

p27 No 51 Sqn's last Nimrod re-located to Waddington on 28 April 1995, but one of its three Nimrod R1s was lost on 16 May 1995.

p35 Shawbury has been chosen as base of the Joint Defence Helicopter School, which will be formed on 1 April 1997 (replacing No 2 FTS) with civilian helicopters (possibly Robinson R44s and Eurocopter Ecureuils).

The last two Hawks based at Chivenor departed on 17 March 1995, but the airfield closed on 23 March.

p36 Locking; closure is proposed, No 1 RS to re-locate to Cosford.

p37 No 618 VGS transferred to Challock by April 1995.

p38 Nos 7 and 9 AEFs were re-equipped with Bulldog T1s in January 1995 and the remaining AEFs are expected to follow during 1995, simultaneously amalgamating with UASs, where appropriate. Bulldog codes are 76-78 for No 7 AEF and 87-89 for No 9 AEF.

p39 The former USAF weapons storage base at Welford was returned to the RAF (parented by Brize Norton) on 31 March 1995 and is being maintained as an active station.

p42 The first Jaguar GR1B, XX748, first flew on 11 January 1995 and was handed-over to the RAF on 24 February.

An order for 14 further Chinooks (and 22 EH101s) was announced on 9 March 1995; nine of the Chinooks will be equipped to carry Special Forces on covert missions and be equipped similarly to the USAF's MH-47E.

p69 Two new grey paint colours have been introduced on RAF aircraft: Camouflage Grey replaces Barley Grey; and Dark Camouflage Grey replaces Dark Sea Grey. Tornado GR1 ZA559 and GR1B ZA490 were the first of this type to be painted experimentally, in May-June 1994, and Jaguar GR1A XZ357 returned to Coltishall on 3 February 1995 after similar treatment at St Athan, others following.

p71 Harrier GR7s (beginning with No 4 Sqn) were due to replace the Operation Grapple Jaguar detachment from August 1995.

p72 Tornado GR1s took-over the Operation Warden deployment on 3 April 1995 when six aircraft of No 617 Sqn left the UK to replace Harriers.

p78 Withdrawal of the RAF's nuclear role (with WE177B bombs) has been brought forward to late-1998, at which time the RN will have three Trident missile armed submarines in operation.

p83 No 19 Sqn, RAF Regiment, disbanded in February 1995 and No 66 has also been withdrawn.

p89 UKADR Sector 1 at Buchan and Sector 2 at Neatishead were disbanded on 31 March 1995. Fighter control throughout the UK's area of responsibility is now directly exercised by the Sector Operations Centre at Bentley Priory.

p92 Saxa Vord's Type 96 radar was switched off for the last time on 31 March 1995.

No 1 Air Control Centre formed at Boulmer on 1 April 1995 as a mobile radar reserve using a Type 93 and the RAF's sole Type 99.

Introduction

In the three years since the previous edition of *abc Royal Air Force*, most reductions in the 'Options for Change' defence review have come to pass. Closely following this has come 'Front Line First' and a host of other cost-saving studies, the effect of which — although less profound — has been to squeeze budgets further and hasten the spread of civilianisation of non-combatant roles throughout the uniformed services. In parallel with the 'downsizing' of the RAF during the first half of the 1990s, two new Groups have formed within Strike Command — one of them replacing the disbanded RAF Germany — and Support Command has been split into two: Logistics Command and Personnel & Training Command.

Consequently, the 1995 edition of *abc Royal Air Force* differs greatly from its predecessor — even more so in detail to reflect the passing of over a dozen operational squadrons, most of which have been reborn as 'shadows' of training units. Illustrative material has also undergone complete revision and expansion, most notably in the inclusion of badges for all numbered squadrons which carry insignia on their aircraft. Conspicuous by their absence are the Buccaneer, Hunter, Phantom and Victor, all of which have been withdrawn after long and meritorious service.

This handbook presents the current organisation and equipment of the RAF and explains its operational tasks and the role of the supporting services which, though remaining on the ground, are no less important than the more visible elements. A secondary function is to record briefly the units, stations and types of aircraft which have ceased to exist during the past three years. Faced with the need to cover a broad spectrum of subjects, the author has sought not to compete with the overlapping, but far more detailed, analyses of certain aspects to be found in companion volumes. *abc Military Aircraft Markings*, *abc Combat Aircraft Recognition*, *abc Air Traffic Control* and *abc Air Band Radio Guide* may therefore be regarded as subjects for further study. *Aficionados* of VHF/UHF radio monitoring and general air traffic procedures will find details in the last two mentioned which — because they are common to both civil and military aviation — can find no place in this publication.

Cuts in RAF strength triggered by disbandment of the Warsaw Pact have proceeded apace during the first half of this decade, in spite of a growing realisation that parts of the world uncomfortably close to the UK have become less stable since relieved of the constraining hand of Communism. Between 1991 and 1994, the RAF shed 14 squadrons, 170 aircraft and 24 bases, its

	IN 1990	'OPTIONS' PLAN	CURRENT PLAN
Tornado GR1	148	112	112
Tornado F3	92	122	100
Phantom	65	0	0
Hawk T1A	72	52	50
Sentry AEW1	0	7	6
Harrier	74	52	52
Jaguar	40	40	40
Buccaneer	30	0	0
Operational helicopter	93	90	90
Tanker/transport	94	83	90
Total	**708**	**558**	**540**

manpower falling from 89,000 in 1990 to 70,000 today. Further reductions are in prospect as a result of the UK defence budget being cut by 14% in real terms between 1992 and 1996, so that by the turn of the century, the RAF will have only 52,200 personnel. Notice has also been served that it will lose its WE177 bombs around 2005 and become a non-nuclear force, yet even conventional weaponry is being neglected, as evidenced by the removal of vital systems from the Tornado GR4 upgrade programme as a result of Treasury penny-pinching.

Operational strength of the RAF is declining from 743 aircraft in 1990, through 595 as envisaged in 'Options for Change' to a new low of 567 plus a squadron or so of extra transport helicopters. These figures, representing only aircraft actually in squadrons and OCUs, reflect a cut of 22 Tornado F3s, 22 Sidewinder-armed Hawks, one Sentry, 36 Tornado GR1s, 22 Harriers, all 30 Buccaneers, all 65 Phantoms, eight Nimrod MR2s and four tanker/ transports.

If anything, commitments have expanded during this recent period of fiscal contraction. In 1995, the RAF had significant policing detachments in Turkey (for northern Iraq), Saudi Arabia (southern Iraq) and Italy (Bosnia), having given up in compensation only its small force in Belize. Unfortunately, as a result of the ineptitude of Western leaders in not acting forcefully in Bosnia, that fiasco will have emboldened dictators from North Korea to Libya. Hopes of a 'New World Order' hailed after the Iron Curtain was torn down have quickly evaporated, making challenges to Western interests just as likely as before Iraq's 1990 invasion of Kuwait. The RAF's prospects for leading a quiet life are not good.

New equipment is, nevertheless, on hand or imminent. Transport is receiving welcome attention, both through recent upgrading of the Chinook helicopter force and imminent replacement of half the Hercules fleet. A little

more distant, the EH 101 helicopter is a further boost to the army's mobility. Technical and political troubles abroad have stretched the Eurofighter 2000 programme with the result that the RAF is no nearer getting its hands on the aircraft than it was when the first edition of this book appeared. Production deliveries begin in 2000 and the first squadron should be operational in 2005.

Eurofighter will replace the Tornado F3 as soon as possible. This long-range interceptor was designed for the Cold War and is at a disadvantage to more agile fighters in the 'policing' type of combat which the RAF is increasingly likely to encounter. Ground elements of air defence have been upgraded in the past few years with the greatly-delayed commissioning of the Improved UK Air Defence Ground Environment and an order for more mobile radars. Equally behind time, the JTIDS air-ground data link is, at last, becoming a reality in Tornado F3s of the Coningsby Wing.

Bolting of the air defence stable door after the Warsaw Pact horse has gone serves to draw attention to the problems of being a middle-ranking power of limited financial means. The programme of air defence improvements now in place was launched in 1977 (and should have been completed 10 years later) to counter long-range bombers passing through the Iceland-UK gap to attack Great Britain from the west.

Opposite:
Last march-past. Recent years have witnessed a spate of unit disbandments and station closures as the RAF adjusts to the post Warsaw Pact world. Closure of RAF Wattisham on a fine autumn late-afternoon in 1992 was but one of many similar events. *Paul Jackson*

Meeting the threat absorbed all available air defence funds, so when the threat abruptly changed, there was no alternative equipment policy. Indeed, the only other interceptor — the Phantom — was withdrawn to save money. If the RAF is wise, it will avoid too highly-specialised aircraft like the Tornado F3 in future.

Versatility will be increased by the new range of 'smart' air-to-ground weaponry being sought for RAF attack aircraft. As well as replacing first-generation laser-guided bombs, there is an urgent need for stand-off weapons dispensers like the MATRA Apache ordered for French Mirage 2000Ds and German Tornados. Despite the lessons of the Gulf War, RAF progress in this area has been extraordinarily leisurely.

As usual, it is the human resources of the RAF which will be required to make up for its shortcomings in material. Aircrew instruction has slowed significantly as a result of front-line reductions, whilst cost-saving cuts in the pilot training programme are merely transferring a greater instructional burden to squadrons, including those with real commitments in 'policing' operations.

The snapshot view of the RAF in 1995 as contained in this volume finds the Service having achieved only the first of the 'smaller, leaner, fitter' objectives set by its political masters when they tightened the purse-strings. Only gradually will equipment programmes fall into line with the realities of World events and the excess of flying personnel be smoothed. Until then, there may be more hard decisions ahead for the RAF.

Above:
Tornado F3 take-off.
Paul Jackson

1 Stations

Closure or abandonment of nine major flying stations in 1992-94 has reduced to 27 the number of locations accommodating operational units or large flying training establishments. In addition, around 50 minor or joint-user aerodromes are employed by the RAF, including the resuscitated Colerne. Major bases are listed below with brief notes on their history and role; the minor aerodromes appear in tabular form. Not included are USAF bases, all of which are officially RAF installations. The parallel draw-down of US military forces has left several major aerodromes devoid of residents — notably Bentwaters/Woodbridge (to RAF 30 September 1993), Upper Heyford (to RAF 30 September 1994) and Alconbury (airfield closed 31 March 1995). A storage depot at Burtonwood reverted to the RAF on 2 June 1993 and the Chicksands communications site will follow on 30 September 1995.

In the following lists, details given immediately following the name are the county (country for overseas bases); distance and direction from the nearest town; heading and length of the principal runway (with any secondary runway in parentheses) — see Chapter 7 for further details; and resident flying units. Where space permits, notable non-flying units are mentioned, but their inclusion is not intended to be comprehensive.

It will be noted that most major stations date from the expansion period of the RAF in the mid/late-1930s. They will be found to have a similar style of building, the most obvious feature of which is the concertina-roofed, Type C hangar, later examples of which lack gables (squared corners) to the roof. A further modification for speed and economy of erection was the C1, in which asbestos replaced much of the brickwork. C1s at Kinloss have recently been re-covered with plastic cladding, presenting an unusual appearance.

In the early-war period, the curved-roof Type J and virtually identical Type K hangars were introduced to simplify construction, examples being found at Coningsby and Lyneham, both dating from 1940. Stations opened in the early- and mid-war years were built with corrugated iron Bellman, Type T or similar hangars. Some, notably T2s, augmented the accommodation at permanent bases and remain in use to this day. Stations which changed function or had two simultaneous roles reflect that in their architecture — a good example being Lossiemouth, which has Types C, J, L and T2 hangars.

The Type L (and similar E) is a medium-sized, blister-shaped hangar for storing dismantled aircraft, its small doors making it useful now only for vehicles. Built at maintenance units (MU), most of the survivors remain, covered by turf.

Another MU hangar was the Type D: tall, like the Type C, but with the J/K's curved roof. Brize Norton and St Athan possess Type Ds, as well as other models. Rarities include the small Type F hangars (with sliding doors in one side, rather than at the ends) at Cranwell (with Bellmans and Cs) and — surviving from World War 1 — Belfast Truss hangars used for equipment storage at Leuchars. Visitors to the Battle of Britain Memorial Flight at Coningsby will note that it is housed in a Type B high-roofed, corrugated iron hangar.

At former V-Bomber stations such as Wittering and Coningsby, the Gaydon Hangar will be seen complementing the older accommodation. First built at Gaydon, this is similar to the J/K types, but constructed of concrete. Later erections for large aircraft have included the Base Hangar at Brize Norton (VC10) and the wire-encircled Sentry Hangar at Waddington. The newest scratch-built station at Mount Pleasant in the Falkland Islands has much original infrastructure, including two unique hangars — one large; one, with an unusually low roof, for helicopters.

MAJOR UK BASES

Aircraft enthusiasts are drawn to aerodromes to pursue their hobby from the outside. The data which follow make no attempt to identify vantage points at airfields. It must suffice to record that in a densely-populated island, most bases have roads from which landing — and even taxying — aircraft can be photographed. The RAF Police need to be vigilant, but co-operation and proof of identity if questioned is normally enough to satisfy the authorities. Damaging of crops to get closer to airfields surrounded by farmland reflects badly on all aviation enthusiasts and is to be deplored.

Collectors of serial numbers are advised below of those bases having hardened aircraft shelters (HAS) in which aircraft are kept when not flying. Other stations can be assumed to keep their aircraft on a flight-line during operating hours — those with large maritime and transport aircraft leaving them outdoors at all times other than when being overhauled.

Enthusiasts should clearly understand that the liberal attitude shown by the authorities towards their hobby in the UK is most definitely **NOT** shared throughout Europe — even in some EU and NATO countries.

MAJOR BASES

● **AKROTIRI** (Cyprus). Southwest of Limassol in British Sovereign Base Area — inaccessible to enthusiasts. 10/28 8,993ft. No 84 Sqn, Wessex HC2. Built 1956 as a strategic base and now major staging post, which was heavily used in connection with 1991 Gulf War. Armament Practice Camp (APC) for RAF Tornado F3s, which resident for three-week rotations, assisted by banner-towing Hawks of No 100 Sqn from Finningley. Wessex provide SAR cover for APC, transport for visiting army detachments and security patrols and occasional support for United Nations. In east of Cyprus, RAF Kingsfield is rudimentary emergency airfield.

● **ALDERGROVE** (Ulster). Sixteen miles west of Belfast. 07/25 9,111ft; 17/35 6,401ft; No 72 Sqn (Wessex HC2); No 230 Sqn (Puma HC1); Queen's UAS and No 13 AEF (Bulldog T1). Northern Ireland's principal airport occupies part of RAF Aldergrove, established in 1918 and previously the home of No 23 MU. The station's main role is now support of Army security patrols, the RAF presence having been boosted with transfer of No 230 Sqn from Germany on 4 May 1992, joining long-term resident, No 72. A detachment of Chinooks is supplied by No 7 Sqn at Odiham. In addition, Army Air Corps residents are No 655 Sqn (Lynx AH7), No 665 Sqn (Lynx AH7 and Gazelle AH1) and No 1 Flight (Islander AL1), whilst the Navy is represented by a detachment of Sea King HC4s of No 707 Sqn from Yeovilton. An RAF Reconnaissance Intelligence Centre processes imagery from the camera-equipped Islanders. SAR duties in Northern Ireland are undertaken by a stand-by Puma.

● **BENSON** (Oxfordshire). Two miles northeast of Wallingford. 01/19 5,981ft. No 60 Sqn (Wessex HC2) for Army support — particularly 5 Airborne Brigade — and including the Wessex Training Flight; London UAS and Oxford UAS (Bulldog T1); No 6 AEF (Chipmunk T10). Opened 1939 and became famous as a photo-reconnaissance base; home of royal flying from May 1946 until The Queen's Flight moved to Northolt in April 1995. Benson received its two UASs and the AEF from Abingdon in July 1992; the Mobile Catering Support Unit from Hullavington later in 1992; and gained the HQ Support Helicopter Force from Gütersloh in April 1993. Since June 1993, it has been the HQ of No 1 Group, previously at Upavon.

● **BRIZE NORTON** (Oxfordshire). Five miles southeast of Burford. 08/26 10,007ft. Military Emergency Diversion Airfield (see Chapter 7). No 10 Sqn (VC10 C1/C1K); No 101 Sqn (VC10 K2/K3/K4); No 216 Sqn (TriStar K1/KC1/C2/C2A); and No 55 (Reserve) Sqn, the tanker/transport OCU (TriStar and VC10). Opened 1937 and used by the Airborne Forces during World War 2; also home to No 6 MU, hangar accommodation of which remains. Major extensions by the USAF from 1950 onwards, when the station housed rotations of B-29s, B-36s, B-47s ad B-52s. Brize reverted to the RAF as a transport base in 1965. Joint Air Transport Establishment, in two Type D hangars on the southeast side, and related Air Movements School have a few training airframes. No 1 Parachute Training School uses Lyneham's Hercules for drops over Weston-on-the-Green, and elsewhere. The 'Falcons' parachute display team (formed 1961) is an element of No 1 PTS. The Air Loadmaster School is another resident and the base is a convenient location for short-notice deployment units in the form of the UK Mobile Air Movements Squadron, No 1 Aeromedical Evacuation Squadron and the Tactical Communications Wing. Brize is the RAF's main strategic transport base with regular TriStar and VC10 C1 services around the Globe.

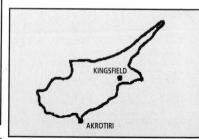

VC10 K2/K3 and recently-received K4s are the main aerial tanker force and are being repainted from hemp to grey. Likewise, the C1 fleet is being given optional tanker capability in C1(K) form. No 55 Sqn was relegated to a ground school in 1994.

● **BRÜGGEN** (Germany). West of Mönchengladbach, adjacent to the Dutch border. 09/27 8,159ft. Nos IX, 14, 17 and 31 Sqn (Tornado GR1). Sole RAF strike/attack base in Germany following disbandment of Laarbruch-based Tornado squadrons. With Geilenkirchen, Laarbruch and Wildenrath, the base was built during the early-1950s to secure air assets from a rapid Warsaw Pact advance by placing them as far west as possible. Opened in May 1953, it has always been associated with strike/attack roles, the Tornado having replaced Jaguars in 1984-85. Former resident, No 431 MU has closed. Aircraft are operated from HAS sites and are difficult to observe from outside the base. With closure of Wildenrath, Brüggen has become the main RAF airhead for Germany, its new passenger terminal handling both military and civilian traffic.

● **COLTISHALL** (Norfolk). Eight miles NNE of Norwich. 04/22 7,500ft. Nos 6, 41 and 54 Sqn (Jaguar GR1A/T2A). Assigned to attack and reconnaissance roles, Jaguars of the Coltishall Wing distinguished themselves in the Gulf War of 1991 and were later based in Turkey to watch over Iraqi Kurdistan and in Italy for protection of the UN force in Bosnia. The base opened as a fighter station in May 1940 and remained thus until Jaguars began arriving in 1974. Jaguars currently operate from a flight-line as their wartime role is to redeploy as reinforcements for the NATO flanks. The Wessex formerly with 'E' Flight of No 22 Sqn were stood-down on 21 July 1994, following establishment of a Sea King flight at Wattisham.

● **CONINGSBY** (Lincolnshire). Eight miles SSW of Horncastle. 08/26 9,000ft. Nos 5 and 29 Sqn, No 56 (Reserve) Sqn/Tornado F3 OCU and F3OEU (all Tornado F3); and Battle of Britain Memorial Flight (Lancaster BI, Hurricane IIC, Spitfire IIA, VB, PR XIX, Dakota C4, Devon C2/2 and Chipmunk T10). The first of three Tornado interceptor bases, Coningsby housed bombers from 1940 until the first Phantoms arrived in 1968. Tornado deliveries began in 1984 and the last Phantom (on completion of a local overhaul) left the base on 16 October 1987. No 56(R) Sqn (formerly No 229 OCU) provides Tornado F3 pilots and navigators and the F3 Operational Evaluation Unit is responsible to the Air Warfare Centre at HQ Strike Command for developing operational procedures and evaluating new equipment. Recent work has been with the JTIDS data link, which is being issued to both the resident

Above:
Fighter line-ups are a rarity in the days of the HAS. Coltishall's Jaguars operate daily from a traditional type of flight-line, here viewed from the control tower. *Paul Jackson*

operational squadrons at Coningsby. These two squadrons operate from HAS sites, but other aircraft use the flight-line. The BBMF hangars are open to visitors on *most* weekdays (telephone 01526 344041).

● **COTTESMORE** (Leicestershire). Five miles northeast of Oakham. 05/23 9,003ft. Trinational Tornado Training Establishment (Tornado GR1/IDS). All conversion training for the interdictor/strike version of Tornado is undertaken at Cottesmore, where the TTTE received its first aircraft in 1980. The unit trains German and Italian students alongside those of the RAF, but crews are posted to other bases (Lossiemouth in the case of the RAF) to learn combat procedures. Tornados from Germany and Italy are included in the Cottesmore fleet, and the base naturally

attracts visiting transport aircraft from those countries. Flying is conducted by the Tornado OCU, comprising 'A', 'B', 'C' and 'S' (Standards) Squadrons, although badges on the aircraft are representative only. TTTE's 200th main course graduated on 19 February 1994. The base opened in August 1938; was used by USAAF transports in 1943-45; and housed both Victor and Vulcan V-Bombers during the 1950s and 1960s. A large parking ramp was amongst the many major construction projects initiated for Tornado operations.

● **CRANWELL** (Lincolnshire). Four miles northwest of Sleaford. 09/27 6,293ft (01/19 4,803ft). No 3 FTS (Tucano T1); RAF College Air Squadron (Bulldog T1). This former Royal Naval Air Service airship station, opened in 1915, is famous as the home of the RAF College, its flying component being No 3 FTS. The school's last Jet Provost left on 29 October 1991, Tucano deliveries having begun in December 1990. Barkston Heath is the principal satellite, but Cranwell North is a grass airfield across the (B1429) road from the main site used by the local gliding club. Interesting architecture includes a variety of hangars and other buildings spanning three-quarters of a century. All future RAF officers pass through Cranwell for at least (since 1979) their 24-week Initial Officer Training course, those from University Air Squadron proceeding to No 3 FTS for flying training. Other elements include the Headquarters University Air Squadrons (with associated Bulldog squadron) and Department of Air Warfare (part of the Air Warfare Centre since July 1993). Engineering trainees of the Department of Special Ground Training — unofficially known as 'No 284 (Training) Sqn' — have a fleet of grounded Hunters in a hangar on the southeast corner of the airfield. The aircraft

are kept notionally airworthy and will be seen taxying from time to time. Cranwell may receive some additional aircraft with the closure of Finningley and Scampton.

● **FINNINGLEY** (South Yorkshire). Five miles southeast of Doncaster. 02/20 8,993ft. No 6 FTS (Dominie T1, Tucano T1, Hawk T1 and Bulldog T1); No 45 (Reserve) Sqn/METS (Jetstream T1); No 100 Sqn (Hawk T1/T1A); Yorkshire UAS (Bulldog T1); and No 9 AEF (Chipmunk T10). Finningley's main role is training of most non-pilot aircrew (navigators, air electronics and air engineer personnel). The last Jet Provosts were withdrawn from service on 14 August 1993, and replaced by a combination of Tucanos (first delivery 6 April 1992) and Hawks (10 September 1992), two of the latter being in the markings of the Joint Forward Air Controllers Standards and Training Unit. No 6 FTS's Basic Navigation Wing comprises No 1 BN Training Sqn (Bulldog and Tucano); No 2 BNTS (Dominie); the Ground School and Officer Training Squadron. The Advanced Navigation Wing includes the Hawk Squadron, Air Navigation Training Squadron (Dominie) and Navigation School Standards Squadron. Also part of the FTS, the Multi-Engine Training Squadron (alias No 45 Sqn since 1 July 1992), converts students from single-engined aircraft and prepares them for flying large transports and maritime aircraft. The civilian airfield at Gamston is used as a satellite by Bulldogs of the FTS, which have blue rudders to differentiate them from the black and yellow striped rudders of YUAS. No 100 Sqn's Hawks provide targets for gunnery and radar training. A former resident, the HQ UK SAR Wing disbanded on 1 December 1992, its elements dispersed to Boulmer and St Mawgan. Opened in 1936, Finningley was mainly a bomber and bomber-training base until the present residents began arriving from 1970 onwards. It was announced in July 1994 that Finningley will close. Likely transfers include Tucanos to Topcliffe; Hawks to Valley/Leeming and Jetstreams and Dominies to Cranwell.

● **KINLOSS** (Grampian). Three miles northeast of Forres. 08/26 7,582ft. Nos 42 (Reserve)/Nimrod OCU, 120, 201 and 206 Sqn (Nimrod MR2); No 663 VGS (Vigilant T1). Long the RAF's principal maritime reconnaissance base, the station became the sole Nimrod MR2 operator on 1 October 1992, when the former No 236 OCU moved up from St Mawgan and simultaneously became No 42 (R) Sqn. However, St Mawgan is retained as a forward operating base. By 1993, the Nimrod pool had been reduced to 26 aircraft, including four in reserve. Some Nimrods carry representative insignia of the three operational squadrons. Opened in 1939, Kinloss has developed strong maritime reconnaissance traditions since 1942, although initially a training base. Across the airfield from the main camp, the Nimrod Major Servicing Unit (formed 1 February 1972) is responsible for overhauls, including the R1s of No 51 Sqn.

● **LAARBRUCH** (Germany). Three miles southwest of Weeze. 10/28 8,012ft. The last of the 'Clutch' bases (Brüggen, Geilenkirchen, Laarbruch and Wildenrath) built with German war reparations, Laarbruch opened in October 1954 and has been involved with strike/attack aircraft ever since. Following transfer or disbandment of its four Tornado GR1/1A squadrons in 1991/92, the station took over Gütersloh's aircraft and received Nos 3 and IV Sqn and their Harrier GR7s in November 1992, followed by No 18 Sqn's Chinook HC1s and Puma HC1s in March 1993. Harriers have been providing a detachment to Incirlik, Turkey, since April 1993 for policing northern Iraq. Conversion of No 18 to HC2 versions of Chinook began with arrival of the first on 1 February 1994. An announcement in July 1994 revealed that Laarbruch will close by 1999, its helicopters transferring to the UK the year before. Harriers are likely to follow suit.

● **LEEMING** (North Yorkshire). Six miles southwest of Northallerton. 16/34 7,520ft. Nos 11 and 25 Sqn (Tornado F3); Northumbrian UAS (Bulldog T1); No 11 AEF (Chipmunk T10); and (from late 1995) No 100 Sqn (Hawk T1/T1A). Dating from 1940, this former bomber station progressed to fighter operations and then flying training before being extensively rebuilt in the

Below:
Brize Norton's two Type D hangars immediately identify the base as a former maintenance unit. Those at St Athan are similar. *Paul Jackson*

Above:
Roads on RAF stations are often named for aircraft types or prominent figures in aviation history. A freer policy obtains at Mount Pleasant, Falkland Islands, where the Hercules of No 1312 Flight live in (Fat) Albert Square and the Police HQ is down Letsby Avenue. *RAF*

late-1980s in preparation for the Tornado. The first squadron, No 11, formed here in July 1988 and the last, No 25, was declared operational in January 1990. In between, No 23 Sqn also flew Tornados, but disbanded on 28 February 1994. Its HAS site was taken over by No 11, which had previously operated from the original hangars.

● **LEUCHARS** (Fife). Four miles northwest of St Andrews. 09/27 8,491ft (04/22 4,803ft). Military Emergency Diversion Airfield (see Chapter 7). Nos 43 and 111 Sqn (Tornado F3); Aberdeen, Dundee and St Andrews UAS (Bulldog T1). The third and last permanent Tornado F3 base re-equipped its resident squadrons during 1989-90 and the era of the Phantom ended here in January 1991 when No 228 OCU disbanded, the final aircraft leaving in April. As a result of the decline in Russian aircraft transiting the UK Air Defence Region, Leuchars became the sole QRA (Fighter) base on 9 January 1992. Soon after, it began increasing the strength of its resident squadrons from 12 to 18 Tornados each, although they currently have 16. Plans to expand other fighter units have been abandoned. Wessex detachment, 'B' Flight of No 22 Sqn, disbanded on 1 April 1993. Leuchars is the oldest of Scotland's military aerodromes, having begun as a balloon station in 1911. A long-standing maritime connection finally terminated with the installation of fighters in 1950.

● **LINTON-ON-OUSE** (North Yorkshire). Eight miles northwest of York. 04/22 6,020ft (10/28 4,394ft). No 1 FTS (Tucano T1); and No 642 VGS

(Vigilant T1). Final operator of the Jet Provost in a pilot-training role, No 1 FTS graduated its last JP course (No 125) on 4 June 1993, having begun conversion to Tucanos in May 1992. The FTS's Topcliffe satellite previously housed Bulldogs of the Royal Navy EFTS, but operations there passed to Hunting Aircraft on 7 July 1993. On that date, the Bulldogs were replaced by civil-registered Slingsby Fireflies of the Joint Elementary Flying Training School, providing 62hr of instruction to Navy students and (as a replacement for Chipmunks of the former EFTS at Swinderby) 54hr to their RAF equivalents. JEFTS moved to Barkston Heath in April 1995. Church Fenton and Dishforth are used as relief landing grounds. Linton is expected to receive Tucanos from No 6 FTS and CFS when they are dispersed by 1996-97, boosting the linked bases' complement of this type to 60. Linton's background is as a bomber base from 1937 and a fighter station postwar, until the arrival of No 1 FTS in 1957.

● **LOSSIEMOUTH** (Grampian). Four miles north of Elgin. 05/23 9,091ft (10/28 6,025ft). Nos 12 and 617 Sqn (Tornado GR1B); No XV (Reserve) Sqn/Tornado Weapons Conversion Unit (Tornado GR1); No 16 (Reserve) Sqn/Jaguar OCU (Jaguar GR1A/T2A); and 'D' Flight of No 202 Sqn (Sea King HAR3). Opened in 1939, 'Lossie' was an RAF training and maintenance base in World War 2, then became a Fleet Air Arm shore station until September 1972. The RAF's last two Buccaneer squadrons (Nos 12 and 208) disbanded here in 1993-94, during which time three Tornado squadrons were installed: No XV from Honington on 1 November 1993; and Nos 12 and 617 from Marham on 7 January and 27 April 1994. The two last-mentioned replace Buccaneers in the maritime strike/attack role with weapons including Sea Eagle anti-ship missiles. Lossiemouth is a busy station, especially during local maritime exercises.

● **LYNEHAM** (Wiltshire). Ten miles southwest of Swindon. 18/36 5,991ft. Nos 24, 30, 47 and 70 Sqn and No 57 (Reserve) Sqn/Hercules OCU (Hercules C1/C1(K)/C3). Home of the entire RAF Hercules force apart from two C1(K) tankers based in the Falkland Islands on rotation, Lyneham opened in 1940 and has been a transport base for all but the first two years of its existence. It sees a variety of foreign visitors. Hercules are operated in a central pool and carry no unit markings. The C-130J variant, ordered for the RAF as (presumably) Hercules C4, will be received from spring 1997. Also resident is the UK Mobile Air Movements Squadron which is responsible for establishing handling facilities at any temporary base adopted as an airhead.

● **MARHAM** (Norfolk). Seven miles southeast of King's Lynn. 06/24 9,140ft (01/19 5,900ft). Nos II and 13 Sqn (Tornado GR1A); No 39 (1 PRU) Sqn (Canberra PR9). Marham opened in April 1937 and maintained a long association with bomber aircraft. Indeed, the last survivors of Britain's V-Bombers, the Victor tankers of No 55 Sqn, were withdrawn there in October 1993. The station is now the RAF's tactical reconnaissance centre. Two Tornado strike squadrons (Nos 27 and 617) have departed and been replaced by a pair of Tornado recce squadrons: No II from Germany in December 1991 and No 13 from Honington on 1 February 1994. In between, No 39 (1 PRU) Sqn arrived from Wyton with its Canberra PR9s on 30 November 1993.

● **MOUNT PLEASANT** (Falkland Islands). 28 miles WSW of Port Stanley. 10/28 8,500ft (05/23 5,000ft). No 78 Sqn (Sea King HAR3 and Chinook HC2); No 1312 Flight (Hercules C1(K)); and No 1435 Flight (Tornado F3). The RAF's newest aerodrome was officially opened on 12 May 1985 to deter Argentina from any further attempts to invade the Falkland Islands. The base has a minimal establishment of four Tornados (which replaced Phantoms in July 1992), two Hercules, two Chinooks and two Sea Kings, but has considerable accommodation and armament stocks for reinforcement attack, interceptor and maritime reconnaissance aircraft flown directly from the UK with tanker support.

● **NORTHOLT** (Greater London). Three miles ENE of Uxbridge. 07/25 5,525ft. No 32 (The Royal) Sqn (BAe 125 CC2/CC3; BAe 146, Wessex HCC4; Gazelle HT3); Northolt Station Flight (Islander CC2/CC2A); and BAe 125/146 OCU. London's military airport was built as a fighter base in 1915 and retained defensive commitments until the end of World War 2, when its present role of VIP transport was adopted. Large aircraft visiting London must land elsewhere because of Northolt's comparatively short runway. Nevertheless, the base handles a multitude of foreign military transport and communications aircraft and during late-1994 was being promoted as a terminal for executive aviation. No 32 Sqn operates the BAe 125 OCU and previously administered the Andover OCU until the last of this type were withdrawn from the unit in March 1995. The Queen's Flight moved from Benson on 1 April 1995 and was integrated with No 32 Sqn.

● **ODIHAM** (Hampshire). Seven miles east of Basingstoke. 10/28 6,027ft. No 7 Sqn (Chinook HC2); No 33 Sqn (Puma HC1); and No 27 (Reserve) Sqn (Chinook/Puma). Odiham is the home of the RAF Support Helicopter Force, which is dedicated to airlifting the army and its equipment at home and overseas. Opened in 1937 — appropriately in Army Co-operation Command — it housed fighter-attack aircraft

during and after World War 2, until becoming a helicopter base in 1960. The runway is kept operational for occasional fixed-wing visitors. The transport helicopter OCU, No 240, became No 27 (Reserve) Sqn on 1 October 1993. During that year, Chinook HC1s were in short supply due to HC2 conversions in the USA, resulting in the units pooling their few remaining Mk 1s. The first Chinook HC2 was delivered to Odiham on 20 May 1993, *en route* to the A&AEE.

● **ST ATHAN** (South Glamorgan). 12 miles southwest of Cardiff. 08/26 5,988ft. University of Wales Air Squadron (Bulldog T1); and No 634 VGS (Viking T1). Despite its two small flying units, St Athan qualifies as a major base by reason of the maintenance activities of its Aircraft Engineering Wing located on the north, west and south of the aerodrome. The Picketston site is used for aircraft scrapping. St Athan supports most front-line aircraft and undertakes modification programmes and major overhauls. In 1991-92 it absorbed the Hawk, Jaguar and Buccaneer work formerly undertaken at Abingdon and VC10 overhauls from Brize Norton. No 4 School of Technical Training, on the eastern side, includes instructional airframes. The base was built for maintenance duties and opened in February 1939, at one time housing Nos 19 and 32 MUs.

● **ST MAWGAN** (Cornwall). Four miles northeast of Newquay. 13/31 8,984ft. Military Emergency Diversion Airfield (see Chapter 7). HQ Flight, No 22 Sqn (Sea King HAR3 and Wessex HC2); Sea King Training Unit (Sea King HAR3). St Mawgan was opened in 1943; closed in July 1947; and later extensively rebuilt for maritime operations beginning in April 1951, resulting in a non-standard layout for an RAF station. The maritime patrol presence ended when the last resident Nimrod left for Kinloss on 9 September 1992, although the base can accept Nimrod detachments for patrol of the southwestern approaches and its HAS site will accommodate detachments of Tornado GR1Bs. In mid-1992, the station received non-flying units prior to the closure of Mount Batten, these being the School

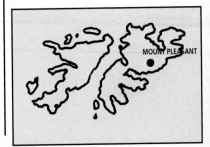

MOUNT PLEASANT

of Combat Survival & Rescue and No 3 Maritime Headquarters. The SKTU moved in from RNAS Culdrose on 2 April 1993 and the SAR Training Unit from Valley is expected in 1996, allowing both to combine as an enlarged Sea King OCU. Currently, the SKTU trains six crews per year, each course lasting 17 weeks. The Aircraft Engineering Squadron (including Helicopter Maintenance Flight for Sea King and Wessex overhauls) and HQ No 22 Sqn arrived from Finningley on 1 October 1992. Despite having few residents, St Mawgan remains open to a steady flow of visiting aircraft, particularly during maritime exercises.

● **SCAMPTON** (Lincolnshire). Five miles north of Lincoln. 05/23 8,990ft. Central Flying School (Bulldog T1, Tucano T1, Hawk T1A); Joint Arms Control Inspection Group (Andover C1[PR]). Scampton was a bomber base from 1936 until 1982, before receiving the CFS HQ in 1984. Primary role is the training of flying instructors, although the Refresher Flying Flight provides courses for pilots returning to the air after a ground tour. Resident Hawks are flown by the 'Red Arrows' aerobatic team. For convenience of servicing and operational considerations, CFS maintains major detachments at other bases: Hawk T1s with the similarly-equipped No 4 FTS at Valley; Gazelle HT3s at No 2 FTS at Shawbury; and various sailplanes at Syerston. Chipmunks are borrowed, as required. A separate unit, the Trade Management Training School has seven Hunters in taxiable condition. Scampton will close in 1996-97 and CFS aircraft will be further dispersed.

● **VALLEY** (Gwynedd). Five miles southeast of Holyhead. 14/32 7,520ft (01/19 5,381ft). No 4 FTS (Hawk T1); 'C' Flight of No 22 Sqn and SAR Training Unit (Wessex HC2). Valley began as a fighter base in 1941 and changed to training 10 years later. This remains its role, with the FTS providing a 100hr Hawk course, including basic weapons training, to pilots selected for fast jets after their Tucano phase. In October 1994, Valley's student throughput increased following disbandment of No 7 FTS at Chivenor. It now comprises Nos 19 (from Chivenor), 74 and 208 Sqn for student instruction; plus the CFS Squadron, responsible for providing instructors. Nearby Mona is used as a relief landing ground. SARTU (formed 1979) trains all rescue helicopter aircrew for at least their basic stage, future Sea King personnel then going to the SKTU at St Mawgan. Valley is the base for aircraft firing missiles at annual camps with the Strike Command Air-to-Air Missile Establishment. (Jindivik, Chukar and Stiletto unmanned targets are provided by Test & Evaluation Establishment, Llanbedr.)

Below:
Leuchars is the only operational RAF station to retain World War 1-style Belfast hangars, although they are no longer used for aircraft storage. A No 100 Sqn Hawk taxies out. *Paul Jackson*

● **WADDINGTON** (Lincolnshire). Four miles south of Lincoln. 03/21 9,000ft. No 8 Sqn and Sentry Training Squadron (Sentry AEW1). No 51 Sqn (Nimrod R1). Opened in 1937, Waddington had a long history as a bomber base which ended in 1984, when an immediate change to Nimrod AEW3s was envisaged. Because of insurmountable problems with the aircraft's radar, it was not until July 1991 that No 8 Sqn re-formed at Waddington in the AEW role — with Sentries. No 51 Sqn and its intelligence-gathering Nimrods arrived from Wyton early in 1995, and is to be joined later in the same year by the Electronic Warfare Operational Support Establishment and its EW Avionic Unit (formed 1 June 1976) which is responsible for special installations, but now has no permanent allocation of aircraft. More interesting to the enthusiast is the broad variety of foreign fighter aircraft which pass through Waddington whilst using the privately-operated (BAe) air combat manoeuvring range over the North Sea. Debrief terminals for the range are located at Waddington, Coningsby, Lakenheath, Leeuwarden, Volkel and Twenthe, with Leeming possibly to follow. The base is also well utilised by overseas visitors to national air defence exercises and by training aircraft from Scampton and elsewhere.

● **WITTERING** (Cambridgeshire). Three miles south of Stamford. 08/26 9,050ft. No 1 Sqn and No 20 (Reserve) Sqn/Harrier OCU (Harrier GR7/T10) With its rear entrance in Leicestershire, this unusually large RAF station (incorporating the former Collyweston airfield) ironically operates STO/VL fighter-bombers. However, there is ample space within the boundary for several training sites on which the Harrier can practise dispersed operations. Opened in 1916, and home to the CFS between the wars, the base received the world's first operational STO/VL combat aircraft in 1969. The initial Harrier GR5 arrived at Wittering on 29 May 1987 and the OCU (formerly No 233) completed upgrading to GR7s in 1994. Two-seat T10s are replacing first-generation Mk4s, having flown their first mission on 1 March 1995 with No 20 (R) Sqn.

Recent stand-downs
● **Abingdon** Closed 31 July 1992. To Army's Royal Logistic Corps as Dalton Barracks; occasional use by Hercules and helicopters for exercises.
● **Belize City** Harrier and Puma flights withdrawn 1993-94.
● **Brawdy** No 1 TWU closed 31 August 1992; Sea King flight (B/202) to Chivenor 1 April 1994.
● **Chivenor** No 7 FTS (Hawk) ceased operations 30 September 1994; station to care & maintenance 1 October 1995, except helicopter flight. To become a Royal Marines base. See list of

minor aerodromes.
● **Church Fenton** No 7 FTS (Tucano) ceased operations March 1992; airfield relegated to relief landing ground.
● **Gütersloh** Airfield closed 30 March 1993; station transferred to Army as Princess Royal Barracks 1 July 1993.
● **Honington** Airfield closed 1 February 1994; station transferred to RAF Regiment.
● **Wattisham** Airfield closed 30 October 1992; transferred to Army Air Corps 1 July 1993. See list of minor aerodromes.
● **Wyton** Airfield closed on transfer of station to HQ Personnel & Training Command; Wyton became subsidiary of Brampton on 1 April 1995.

MINOR AERODROMES
RAF flying activities of a minor nature are undertaken at the aerodromes listed below. The installations themselves are not necessarily small, as some units are lodged at civil airports. Only main runway details are given and installations which are not wholly RAF or at which it is a lodger are indicated by an asterisk.

Some research units are included, and it may be useful to detail the changes which have taken place in R&D establishments over the past few years as they have been re-grouped and made more financially accountable. All are now subordinate to the Defence Evaluation & Research Agency, which was formed on 1 April 1995.

Defence Evaluation & Research Agency
incorporating
● 1. DRA (Defence Research Agency) Formed 1 April 1991, replacing Royal Aerospace Establishment, Royal Signals Research Establishment and Army/Navy equivalents and also including:
Air Flight Ranges Division (T&EE — Test & Evaluation Establishments at West Freugh, Aberporth, Llanbedr and Larkhill)
Land Systems Division (P&EE Proof & Evaluation Establishment ranges at Eskmeals, Pendine, Lavington, Shoeburyness and Foulness)
● 2. DT&EO (Defence Test & Evaluation Organisation) Formed 1 April 1995 (out of Directorate General of Test and Evaluation, formed 1 April 1992), including:
A&AEE (Aircraft & Armament Evaluation Establishment) and its subordinate ETPS (Empire Test Pilots' School)
● 3. Chemical & Biological Defence Establishment at Porton Down
● 4. Centre of Defence Analysis at West Byfleet (P&EE, C&BDE and CDA have no flying units, but some possess static aircraft.)

● **Aberporth***	(Dyfed)	08/26 3,002ft	T&EE
● **Arbroath***	(Tayside)	08/26 3,900ft	No 662 VGS (Viking T1)
● **Barkston Heath**	(Lincs)	06/24 6,000ft	Joint EFTS
● **Boscombe Down***	(Wilts)	06/24 10,537ft	Strike/Attack Operational Evaluation Unit (Harrier GR7, Tornado GR1 and Jaguar T2A) A&AEE, ETPS and DE&RA
● **Boulmer**	(Northumberland)	Nil	A/202 Sqn (Sea King HAR3)
● **Bournemouth***	(Dorset)	08/26 6,030ft	No 2 AEF (Chipmunk T10)
● **Cambridge***	(Cambs)	05/23 6,447ft	Cambridge UAS (Bulldog T1) and No 5 AEF (Chipmunk T10)
● **Catterick***	(N Yorks)	Grass	No 645 VGS (Viking T1)
● **Chetwynd**	(Salop)	Grass	RLG for Shawbury
● **Chivenor**	(Devon)	10/28 6,012ft	B/No 202 Sqn (Sea King HAR3)
● **Church Fenton**	(N Yorks)	06/24 5,774ft	RLG for Linton-on-Ouse
● **Colerne**	(Wilts)	07/25 5,800ft	Bristol UAS (Bulldog), and No 3 AEF (Chipmunk T10)
● **Cosford**	(Salop)	06/24 3,770ft	Birmingham UAS (Bulldog T1) and No 633 VGS (Vigilant T1)
● **Decimomannu***	(Sardinia)	17/35 9,810ft	RAF Support Unit
● **Dishforth**	(N Yorks)	16/34 6,096ft	RLG for Linton-on-Ouse
● **Edinburgh***	(Lothian)	07/25 8,400ft	E Lowlands UAS (Bulldog T1) and No 12 AEF (Chipmunk T10)
● **Exeter***	(Devon)	08/26 6,834ft	No 4 AEF (Chipmunk T10)
● **Glasgow***	(Strathclyde)	05/23 8,720ft	Glasgow & Strathclyde UAS (Bulldog T1)
● **Goose Bay**	(Canada)	08/26 11,050ft	Tornado detachment
● **Halton**	(Bucks)	Grass	No 613 VGS (Vigilant T1)
● **Henlow**	(Beds)	Grass	No 616 VGS (Vigilant T1)
● **Hullavington***	(Wilts)	05/23 4,000ft	Nos 621 and 625 VGS (Viking T1)
● **Kenley**	(Kent)	Grass	No 615 VGS (Viking T1)
● **Kirknewton***	(Lothian)	Grass	No 661 VGS (Viking T1)
● **Leconfield***	(Humberside)	Helicopters	E/202 Sqn (Sea King HAR3)
● **Lt Rissington***	(Glos)	05/23 4,900ft	No 637 VGS (Vigilant T1)
● **Llanbedr***	(Gwynedd)	18/36 7,500ft	T&EE
● **Manston***	(Kent)	11/29 9,029ft	No 1 AEF (Chipmunk T10) and No 617 VGS (Viking T1)
● **Mona**	(Gwynedd)	04/22 5,466ft	RLG for Valley
● **Newton**	(Notts)	Grass	E Midlands UAS (Bulldog T1) and No 7 AEF (Chipmunk T10)
● **North Front**	(Gibraltar)	09/27 6,000ft	Temporary detachments
● **Predannack***	(Cornwall)	05/23 5,950ft	No 626 VGS (Viking T1)
● **Samlesbury***	(Lancs)	07/25 4,934ft	No 635 VGS (Vigilant T1)
● **Sealand**	(Cheshire)	Grass	No 631 VGS (Viking T1)
● **Sek Kong***	(Hong Kong)	Helicopters	No 28 Sqn (Wessex HC2)
● **Shawbury**	(Salop)	01/19 6,018ft	No 2 FTS (Gazelle HT3 and Wessex HC2) and No 8 AEF (Chipmunk T10)
● **South Cerney**	(Glos)	Grass	No 625 VGS (Viking T1)
● **Stornoway***	(Hebrides)	18/36 7,612ft	Reserve interceptor base
● **Swansea***	(W Glam)	04/22 4,829ft	No 636 VGS (Viking T1)
● **Swanton Morley**	(Norfolk)	Grass	No 611 VGS (Viking T1)
● **Syerston**	(Notts)	07/25 5,900ft	Air Cadets' Central Gliding School (Vigilant T1, Valiant T1, Viking T1, Janus C) and No 644 VGS (Vigilant T1)
● **Ternhill***	(Salop)	05/23 3,215ft	No 632 VGS (Vigilant T1)
● **Topcliffe***	(N Yorks)	03/21 6,027ft	JEFTS
● **Upavon***	(Wilts)	Grass	No 622 VGS (Viking T1)
● **Wattisham***	(Suffolk)	05/23 7,490ft	B/202 Sqn (Sea King HAR3)

● West Freugh*	(Dumfries)	06/24 5,997ft	T&EE
● West Malling*	(Kent)	07/25 6,000ft	No 618 VGS (Viking T1)
● Wethersfield*	(Essex)	10/28 9,088ft	No 614 VGS (Viking T1)
● Wideawake	(Ascension)		Staging post to Falklands
● Woodvale	(Merseyside)	04/22 4,754ft	Liverpool UAS & Manchester UAS (Bulldog T1) and No 10 AEF (Chipmunk T10)

RLG — Relief Landing Ground. Usually parented by a training unit to reduce circuit congestion at the main base.

Recent changes and notes

● Bedford	DRA ceased operations here on 31 March 1994; most aircraft transferred to Boscombe Down.
● Binbrook	no longer houses RAF units, following disbandment of No 643 VGS.
● Catterick	transferred to the Army on 30 June 1994, but an RAF lodger unit remains.
● Church Fenton	became an RLG in April 1992; the airfield is retained by the RAF, but the camp has been sold.
● Colerne	(Army base since 1 April 1976), but RAF returned as lodger and began operations late in 1992; control zone was officially activated on 6 October 1993.
● Elvington	lost its RLG status on 25 March 1992 and is no longer used by the RAF.
● Farnborough	DRA ceased operations here on 23 March 1994; most aircraft transferred to Boscombe Down.
● Filton	RAF units vacated this BAe aerodrome early in 1992 for Hullavington.
● Gatow	Station Flight (Chipmunk T10) disbanded 30 June 1994; transferred to German control on 7 September 1994 as new site for *Luftwaffe* Museum.
● Hullavington	closed on 31 March 1993 and passed to Army control; two gliding schools remain as lodger units.
● Machrihanish	closed on 31 March 1995.
● Stornoway	may close as a reserve base for Nos 11 and 111 Sqn.
● Swanton Morley	is to close in 1995.
● Swinderby	closed on 17 December 1993.
● Upavon	transferred to the Army as Trenchard Lines on 30 June 1993; gliding school remains as a lodger unit.
● West Malling	is scheduled for closure.
● West Raynham	closed 1 June 1994.
● Weston-super-Mare	lost No 621 VGS to Hullavington in 1993.
● Wildenrath	closed 30 October 1992.

Below:
RAF College, Cranwell, is the focal point of RAF officer training. *Paul Jackson*

WEAPONS RANGES

Cowden	Humberside
Donna Nook	Lincolnshire
Garvey Island	Highland (1)
Holbeach	Lincolnshire
Luce Bay	Dumfries & Galloway (2)
Nordhorn	Germany
Otterburn	Northumberland (3)
Pembrey	Dyfed
Rosehearty	Grampian
Spadeadam	Cumbria (3)
South Uist	Hebrides (4)
Tain	Highland
Wainfleet	Lincolnshire

Notes:
(1) Used for live bombing
(2) Barges as sea targets
(3) Time-expired aircraft used as targets
(4) RAF and Army Rapier SAM firing

Recent Changes
• **Jurby** Closed 6 July 1993.

MINOR AERODROMES AND RANGES

2 Flying units

In spite of force reductions, the number of RAF squadrons has fallen only slightly during the first half of the 1990s to 57. However, that has been achieved by increasing the quantity of Reserve Squadrons which form the alternative identity of Operational Conversion Units (OCU). The rush of Reserve Squadron allocations and re-allocations during 1991-93 was accompanied in some cases by disbandment of numbered OCUs. For example, the former No 242 OCU is now 'No 57 (Reserve) Sqn/The Hercules OCU'. A variety of supporting units provide the RAF with aircrew; test equipment and new tactics; and give air experience to possible future RAF personnel in the affiliated youth organisations. It is logical to view first the upper structures of the RAF.

Overall control of the RAF is vested in the Air Force Board, subject, of course, to political directives from the government of the day. Beneath Board level, the structure of Commands has altered greatly in recent years. RAF Germany no longer exists as a separate entity, having been absorbed into Strike Command but, by way of indirect replacement, Personnel & Training Command and Logistics Command were formed in 1994 to replace Support Command. In this chapter, the squadrons and other elements of Strike Command are listed first, followed by Personnel & Training Command. No aircraft are operated by Logistics Command.

STRIKE COMMAND (HQ: High Wycombe, Bucks) RAFSC is responsible for all combat and operational support roles in all theatres. Formed on 30 April 1968, it is commanded by an Air Chief Marshal who wears the dual 'hats' of AOC-in-C Strike Command (AOCinC STC) and NATO's C-in-C Allied Air Forces North-West Europe. The latter is a new command formed on 1 July 1994 from the C-in-C's original United Kingdom Air Forces (UKAIR) at High Wycombe and Allied Air Forces Northern Europe (AFNORTH) in Norway. (It is subordinate to the tri-service Allied Forces NWE, also at High Wycombe, as is its counterpart Allied Naval Forces NWE.)

Since 10 April 1975, STC has been wholly committed to NATO as one of its four Major Subordinate Commands, although its HQ was not fully 'internationalised' with allied personnel (as is normal with a NATO HQ) until 1987. Most assets are assigned to NATO's Allied Command Europe, but some were earmarked for Supreme Allied Commander Atlantic. Under the 'Options for Change' force reductions, STC is being cut from its 1990 peak of 800 aircraft and 49,000 military and 5,000 civilian personnel. It is divided into five flying Groups and several directly attached units:

● **No 1 Group** (HQ: Benson, Oxon) administering over-land strike/attack, reconnaissance and army support bases. The Group was responsible for tankers and transports until these were transferred to No 38 Group in November 1992. Its HQ was at Upavon prior to the station being transferred to the Army. The present quarters were occupied in June 1993.

● **No 2 Group** (HQ: Rheindahlen, Germany) controls RAF assets in Germany. Re-formed on 1 April 1993 out of RAF Germany; also responsible for the RAF detachment at the NATO air combat range at Decimomannu, Sardinia, and the weapons range at Nordhorn. No 2 Group aircraft are dedicated directly to Allied Air Forces Central Europe following disbandment of the intermediate 2nd Allied Tactical Air Force on 24 June 1993. (2nd ATAF — which was led by the RAF officer commanding RAFG — controlled all Allied aircraft in the upper half of Central Europe. It passed to German control, briefly, from 7 April 1993 until disbandment.) HQ RAFG officially closed on 30 June 1993. RAFG's own multi-role Maintenance Unit, No 431 MU at Brüggen, closed on 31 March 1993. The Group had 8,885 personnel in April 1992, but only 6,200 by April 1995. It is scheduled to disband on 30 March 1996 and become a detached element of No 1 Group. Laarbruch will close by 1999 after withdrawal of at least its helicopter squadron.

● **No 11 Group** (HQ: Stanmore, London) which has all air defence assets, including interceptors and AEW aircraft.

● **No 18 Group** (HQ: Northwood, London) responsible for maritime patrol, maritime strike attack and SAR.

● **No 38 Group** (HQ: High Wycombe, Bucks) for tanker and transport aircraft. Re-formed 1 November 1992 with elements of No 1 Group. Establishment of No 38 Group partly regularised the previous situation under which the tankers and transports of No 1 Group were controlled from High Wycombe and not Group HQ. However, No 38's status is still anomalous as the Senior Air Staff Officer of Strike Command wears the second 'hat' of C-in-C No 38 Group. Also controls Ascension Island staging post.

NETHERLANDS

NORDHORN RANGE

LAARBRUCH

BELGIUM

BRÜGGEN

GERMANY

LUXEMBOURG

FRANCE

● **MATO** Military Air Traffic Organisation (HQ: Uxbridge, London) No aircraft, although of Group status.

Direct reporting elements are the Air Warfare Centre and overseas squadrons outside Germany. The latter are provided by Strike Command but controlled operationally by the local Headquarters of British Forces, all of which report directly to the tri-service Chief of Defence Staff. They are HQBF Cyprus, HQBF Falkland Islands, HQBF Gibraltar and HQBF Hong Kong. A further command, HQBF Belize, disbanded in 1994.

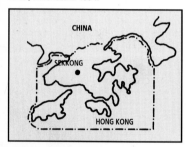

ROYAL AIR FORCE SQUADRONS

Most squadrons can trace their ancestry to World War 1 — or before — and many are now approaching their 80th anniversaries. Numbering of Royal Flying Corps squadrons started at 1, but a second series for strategic bomber squadrons was begun in February 1917 at 100. When the Royal Naval Air Service joined with the RFC on 1 April 1918 to form the RAF, its squadrons had 200 added to their numbers. The result is a group of maritime-related units currently between 201 and 208, whilst No 216 remembers No 16 Squadron, RNAS, by calling itself 'two-sixteen' squadron.

European escapee and Commonwealth squadrons of World War 2 were numbered 300-358 and 400-490, so when an unused number was required in 1966 for a joint RAF-Royal Navy unit, 360 was chosen. This, the RAF's youngest squadron, equipped with Canberra T17s, disbanded in October 1994. The 500 and 600 series were begun by Reservist and Auxiliary squadrons in the 1920s and 1930s and extended during World War 2. First to encroach upon the series previously reserved for the Auxiliaries was No 617 Sqn, the famed 'Dam Busters', which exists to this day. The highest number was No 695. Squadrons of Balloon Command were numbered in the 900s, allowing for naval units in the 700s and 800s.

Flights standardised on the 1300, 1400 and 1500 and 1600 series (followed by naval squadrons in the 1700s and 1800s) and continued into the 1900s for army air observation post units. Whereas most other types of unit have been numbered upwards from 1, Operational Conversion Units began at No 226 OCU, formed on 15 August 1946. The choice of number resulted from the use of 1-200 for Operational Training Units and reservation of 201-225 for Advanced Flying Schools.

Squadrons are formed and disbanded as required by re-equipment programmes and almost all have spent at least some time in limbo. Policy for re-forming units is, broadly, to select the disbanded squadron with the greatest accumulated service, although historical precedent is sometimes allowed influence, to the extent that famous fighter squadrons are perpetuated in that role whenever possible. The NATO forces build-up of the 1980s reached its culmination for the RAF on 1 January 1990 when No 13 Sqn was re-formed. Following unification of Germany in October 1990 and disbandment of the Warsaw Pact in the following year, NATO air forces have been reduced in size and it is unlikely that any more defunct squadrons will be revived.

As a means of perpetuating long-serving squadrons made redundant by the run-down of the RAF, many of their 'number-plates' were assigned to OCU and FTSs as their 'Reserve Squadrons'. The practice is not new, having begun in 1955, but the principle was extended from 1991 onwards by allowing non-combatant units to qualify for a squadron number. Hitherto, OCUs which would have put one or more squadrons into the front line (crewed by instructors) in wartime were assigned a Reserve Squadron number — usually called a 'shadow squadron' — and often applied the squadron's markings to their aircraft. Those OCUs which would split their aircraft and personnel to reinforce several existing squadrons had no requirement for a Reserve identity.

In the listing which follows, data given includes unit number, badge (for numbered squadrons), codes used, base, attached command and group, current aircraft type, unit establishment and role. Badge details for other units are given only in sufficient detail to differentiate units operating the same aircraft type and should not be assumed to describe the complete insignia. 'Marking' indicates that a squadron's aircraft carry a device instead of its badge — for example, No 6 Sqn's can-opener. Several combat squadrons adorn their aircraft with both badge and a secondary means of identification, which is often placed about the fuselage roundel in the form of an arrowhead or coloured rectangle (the latter sometimes known as 'fighter bars' or, if appropriate, a 'checkerboard'). Unit establishment does not always conform exactly to the number of aircraft actually on the squadron at any given time.

STRIKE COMMAND AND RAF GERMANY

Note: For ease of reference, this list also includes the Reserve Squadrons of Personnel & Training Command.

No 1 Sqn Wittering (Strike/1 Group), Harrier GR5 (13) and T10 (1), battlefield air interdiction/close air support. Codes: 01-14. Badge: the number '1' with yellow wings.
Formed with balloons on 13 May 1912, No 1 became the world's first operational STO/VL squadron when converted to Harriers in 1969. The considerably upgraded Harrier GR5 was introduced in November 1988 and No 1 became operational with the variant 12 months later. Night-capable Harrier GR7s were then substituted and the squadron flew its first mission with the new aircraft on 2 June 1992.

No II Sqn Marham (Strike/1 Group), Tornado GR1A (13), tactical reconnaissance and attack. Codes: A-Z (including II). Badge: a Wake Knot flanked by white triangles.
Formed the same day as its predecessor, No II claims to be the oldest RAF unit equipped from the outset with aircraft. Tornados were received in September 1988 and the squadron moved from Germany to Marham on 3 December 1991.

No 3 Sqn Laarbruch (Strike/2 Group), Harrier GR7 (13 increasing to 18; plus one T10), battlefield air interdiction/close air support. Codes: AA-AZ. Badge: a blue and pink Cockatrice.
In Germany since April 1945, the squadron received Harriers in 1972 and was first in RAFG with the GR5 when it began to equip in March 1989. Replacement GR7s arrived from November 1990 and No 3 moved from Gütersloh to Laarbruch on 16 November 1992.

No IV Sqn Laarbruch (Strike/2 Group), Harrier GR7 (13 increasing to 18; plus one T10), battlefield air interdiction/close air support. Codes: CA-CZ. Badge: a lightning flash dividing black and red fields.
Having brought the first Harrier GR1s to Germany in 1970, No IV was first with the new GR7, acceptances of which began in September 1990.

Below:
Combat units invariably wear nose colours, such as No 56(R) Sqn's red and white checks, in addition to a badge on the fin. The aircraft were participating in a rehearsal for the abortive 75th anniversary flypast at Marham. *Paul Jackson*

Transfer of the Harrier force from Gütersloh to Laarbruch brought the unit to its present base on 27 November 1992. In April 1993, the Laarbruch wing established a detachment at Incirlik, Turkey, to patrol northern Iraq. Its aircraft are painted grey overall and carry codes WA-WZ, indicating Operation Warden.

No 5 Sqn Coningsby (Strike/11 Group), Tornado F3 (14), air defence. Codes: CA-CZ. Badge: a yellow V on a green maple leaf, flanked by red bars.
Based mainly overseas with fighters until it became a Lightning unit at Binbrook in 1965, No 5 re-formed with Tornados on 1 January 1988 as the second squadron thus equipped. The Coningsby Wing — in which No 5 is partnered by No 29 — is having its aircraft equipped with the Joint Tactical Information Distribution System (JTIDS) data link.

No 6 Sqn Coltishall (Strike/1 Group), Jaguar GR1A (14) and T2A (3), battlefield and counter-air interdiction/close air support. Codes: EA-EZ. Marking: a red, winged can-opener.
Optimised for rapid overseas deployment as a Regional Reinforcement Squadron or in support of the Allied Command Europe Mobile Force, No 6 has flown Jaguars since October 1974. The Coltishall wing, of which it is the senior member, established a detachment at Gioia del Colle, Italy, in July 1993 for patrols over Bosnia.

No 7 Sqn Odiham (Strike/1 Group), Chinook HC2 (18), helicopter support (plus two Gazelle HT3s, liaison). Codes: EA-EZ (Gazelle A). Badge: the constellation of Ursa Major on a blue disc.
After a career as diverse as bombing and provision of target facilities, No 7 re-formed at Odiham on 1 September 1982 as the home-based Chinook squadron, tasked primarily with supporting the army in medium-lift roles. The squadron's first HC2 version of the Chinook (the second conversion from HC1) was delivered on 10 September 1993. Two Chinooks are detached to Aldergrove. The Gazelle is dark green overall.

No 8 Sqn Waddington (Strike/11 Group), Sentry AEW1 (6), airborne early warning. Codes: nil. Badge: an Arabian dagger.
NATO's last piston-engined front-line aircraft were withdrawn on 30 June 1991 when No 8 disbanded as a Shackleton unit at Lossiemouth. It re-formed at Waddington the following day with long-awaited new equipment and was formally committed to NATO on 1 July 1992. Crews are provided by the co-located Sentry Training Squadron (formed 1 June 1990). Since then, No 8 has been heavily committed to supporting the NATO AEW patrols over Bosnia. One of the squadron's aircraft, ZH107 has been involved in trials of the JTIDS data link.

No IX Sqn Brüggen (RAFG), Tornado GR1 (13), strike/attack. Codes: AA-AZ. Badge: a green bat.
A bomber unit since 1924, this squadron re-formed at Honington on 1 June 1982 as the first operational user of the Tornado GR1 and joined RAFG on 1 October 1986. It has added the BAe Alarm anti-radar missile to its weaponry for defence-suppression missions and became the first RAF unit declared to NATO with this capability on 1 January 1993.

No 10 Sqn Brize Norton (Strike/38 Group), VC10 C1/C1(K) (13), strategic transport. Codes: nil. Badge: an arrow with red wings.
Appropriately, No 10 Sqn equipped with VC10s in July 1966 and is engaged in flying personnel and freight throughout the world on scheduled and unscheduled services. All of its 13 aircraft are being converted to C1(K) tankers with underwing pods, this variant having begun its first operational mission on 19 June 1993 when deployed to the Arabian Gulf in support of Operation Jural over southern Iraq.

No XI Sqn Leeming (Strike/11 Group), Tornado F3 (17), air defence. Codes: DA-DZ. Badge: two black eagles.

The first F3 squadron at Leeming formed on 1 July 1988 and became operational on 1 November. It is assigned to NATO's SACLANT for defence of maritime assets, although its forward base at Stornoway may be abandoned by the RAF.

No 12 Sqn Lossiemouth (Strike/18 Group), Tornado GR1B (13), maritime strike/attack. Codes: FA-FZ. Badge: a fox's mask in brown and white with red detailing.

Formed on 1 October 1969 as the RAF's first Buccaneer squadron, No 12 disbanded at Lossiemouth 24 years later. Simultaneously (1 October 1993) No 27 Squadron at Marham was given the No 12 number-plate and began exchanging its Tornado GR1s for GR1Bs capable of launching the BAe Sea eagle anti-ship missile. Still far from fully reconverted, No 12 transferred to Lossiemouth on 7 January 1994.

No 13 Sqn Marham (Strike/1 Group), Tornado GR1A (13), tactical reconnaissance/conventional attack. Codes: A-Z. Badge: a lynx's face in black and white, flanked by blue bars edged in yellow.

This former Canberra PR9 squadron was revived on 1 January 1990 as the second and last Tornado recce unit. Plans to concentrate most RAF recce assets at Marham resulted in it transferring to this station on 1 February 1994.

No 14 Sqn Brüggen (Strike/2 Group), Tornado GR1 (13), strike/attack. Codes: BA-BZ. Badge: a red cross on a white disc, yellow wings and six blue diamonds.

In Germany since 1946, the squadron has held its current role with Canberras, Phantoms, Jaguars and (from 1 November 1985) Tornados. No 14 was first to receive the JP233 airfield-denial weapon and during the latter part of 1993 gained most of the RAF Tornados capable of carrying the TIALD laser designator.

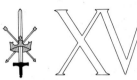

No XV (Reserve) Sqn Lossiemouth (Strike/1 Group), Tornado GR1 (22), training. Codes: TA-TZ. Marking: 'XV' in white and TWCU badge of a sword, gold crown and crossed arrows.

Released from its NATO commitment as a Tornado squadron at Laarbruch on 31 December 1991, the unit returned to the air on 1 April 1992 as the 'shadow' identity of the Tornado Weapons Conversion Unit, displacing No 45 (Reserve) Sqn. As a consequence of closure plans for Honington, No XV relocated to Lossiemouth on 1 November 1993.

No 16 (Reserve) Sqn Lossiemouth (Strike/1 Group), Jaguar GR1A (6) and T2A (4), training. Codes: A-Z. Markings: 'The Saint' and crossed keys, both in yellow on black discs; Lossiemouth tartan on fin RWR housing.

First of the Tornado GR1 squadrons to disappear, No 16 disbanded at Laarbruch on 11 September 1991. On 1 November 1991, No 226 OCU became No 16(R) Sqn and continued its task of training Jaguar pilots for the Coltishall Wing. Fin markings of Lumsden tartan were gradually replaced from February 1994 onwards by the local pattern.

No 17 Sqn Brüggen (Strike/2 Group), Tornado GR1 (13), strike/attack. Codes: CA-CZ. Badge: a red gauntlet on a black/white shield.

No 17 Sqn — 'The Black Knights' — has been in Germany since 1956 and in the strike/attack role from 1970. Phantoms and then Jaguars gave way to Tornados on 1 March 1985.

No 18 Sqn Laarbruch (Strike/2 Group) Chinook HC2 (6), Puma HC1 (5) and one Gazelle HT3, helicopter support. Codes: BA-BZ. Badge: red Pegasus on a black disc.

No 18 gained helicopter experience in Germany for most of the years between 1965 and 1980. Re-formed with Chinooks at Odiham on 24 February 1982, it was diverted for service in the Falklands War two months later and did not begin returning to Gütersloh, Germany, until 21 April 1983, the official consolidation date being 6 August 1983. On 30 April 1992, the unit absorbed some of No 230 Sqn's Pumas, subsequently adjusting its strength to five of each main type, plus (from early-1992) a single Gazelle for communications. No 18 was the last RAF squadron to leave Gütersloh, on 17 March 1993. Its first HC2 Chinook was received on 1 February 1994. No 18 will return to the UK in 1997.

No 19 (Reserve) Sqn, No 4 FTS Valley (P&T Command), Hawk T1/T1A (24) training. Codes: PA-PZ. Badge: a red and green dolphin within yellow wings.

Disbanded with Phantom FGR2s at Wildenrath on 9 January 1992, No 19 re-formed with Hawks on 1 September that year, replacing No 63 Sqn as one of the reserve elements of No 7 FTS at Chivenor. When that unit, disbanded on 30 September 1994, No 19 transferred to Valley to become the identity of the CFS Squadron of No 4 FTS.

• **No 20 (Reserve) Sqn** Wittering (Strike/1 Group) Harrier GR7/T10 (15), training. Codes: A-Z. Markings: A black eagle before a yellow, rising sun, flanked by blue/red/white/black/blue bars; also No 233 OCU badge of a black and grey

wildcat's head.

Disbanded as a Tornado GR1 unit at Laarbruch in May 1992, the squadron was assigned to replace No 233 OCU on 1 September 1992 as the Harrier training unit. The first GR7 versions of Harrier were received in January 1993 to supplant GR5s and the last two GR3s were disestablished on 31 March 1994. Operations with the T10 began on 1 March 1995; seven will have replaced all T4/T4As by late 1995.

• **No 22 Sqn** St Mawgan (Strike/18 Group) Wessex HC2 and Sea King HAR3, search and rescue. Codes: nil. Badge: A black letter 'π' and white Maltese Cross on a black disc.

Officially assigned to rescuing downed airmen, the RAF's SAR force is heavily involved with civilian duties. No 22 Sqn is being reduced in size and converting from Wessex to Sea Kings, the situation by 1996 being three flights in the southern UK, complementing a further three with No 202 Sqn. 'A' Flight at Chivenor converted from Wessex to Sea Kings on 1 April 1994 (receiving aircraft of the simultaneously-disbanded B/202 at Brawdy; 'B' Flight at Wattisham formed on 18 July 1994 with Sea Kings; and 'C' Flight at Valley converts to Sea Kings in June 1996. Of the components no longer extant, 'E' Flight disbanded with Wessex at Coltishall on 21 July 1994 and the previous 'B' Flight with Wessex at Leuchars disbanded on 1 April 1993. No 22 also administers the SAR Training Unit at Valley, this due to move to St Mawgan and become part of the Sea King OCU in 1996.

• **No 24 Sqn** Lyneham (Strike/38 Group) Hercules C1/C1(K)/C3 (14), transport. Codes: nil. Badge: not worn.

No 24 has a long tradition of transport operations, including VIP/VVIP flying during World War 2. On 5 January 1968 it left its Hastings at Colerne and moved to Lyneham to begin receiving Hercules. Its specialities are route flying and aerial tanking, for which it detaches crews to No 1312 Flight in the Falkland Islands. Aircraft are taken from the Lyneham pool as required for individual tasks.

Opposite top:
A Harrier GR7 taxies into its hide during a field exercise. No 2 Group Harriers are spending more time in the UK because of flying restrictions imposed by the German Government. *Paul Jackson*

No 25 Sqn Leeming (Strike/11 Group) Tornado F3 (17), air defence. Codes: FA-FZ. Badge: A grey hawk alighting on a gauntlet.
One of the RAF's traditional fighter units, No 25 was in the less colourful world of surface-to-air missiles between 1963 and 1 October 1989, when its 'number-plate' was transferred to a Tornado squadron forming at Leeming. It became operational on 1 January 1990.

No 27 (Reserve) Sqn Odiham (Strike/1 Group) Chinook HC2 (6), Puma HC1 (5), training. Codes: FA-FZ. Badge: A green elephant on a yellow disc, flanked by red bars.
Long associated with bombing — most recently with Vulcans and Tornados — No 27 disbanded on 30 September 1993. It turned to a different role on 1 October 1993 when the helicopter training unit at Odiham, No 240 OCU, became No 27 (Reserve) Sqn. The OCU had temporarily ceased Chinook training in June 1992, but when first Mk 2s became available, the Chinook Flight was re-formed on 1 January 1994. In fact, conversion of Mk 1 crews to the new aircraft had begun in November 1993, and until May 1994 No 27 borrowed its Chinook HC2s from co-located No 7 Sqn. *Ab initio* conversion courses began in July 1994.

No 28 Sqn Sek Kong (Strike/direct reporting) Wessex HC2 (7), army support. Codes A-Z. Badge: Pegasus.
This unit has been Hong Kong's helicopter squadron since 1 March 1968 and was resident in the colony with fighters between 1949 and 1966. It began replacing Whirlwinds by the current equipment in January 1972. Helicopters are used to transport border security patrols, assist the local police and undertake the regular tasks of SAR and medical evacuation. Since 1917, No 28 has spent three months (non-operational) in the UK and it is expected to disband in 1997, when Hong Kong returns to Chinese control.

No **29 Sqn** Coningsby (Strike/11 Group) Tornado F3 (14), air defence. Codes: BA-BZ. Badge: A red eagle preying on a yellow buzzard.
A dozen years with Phantoms ended for No 29 Sqn with disbandment on the last day of March 1987. On 1 May 1987 it re-formed at Coningsby as the first Tornado F3 squadron and became operational on 1 November. It is assigned to SACLANT for support of maritime operations and earmarked for deployment outside the NATO area, if required in support of UK interests.

No 30 Sqn Lyneham (Strike/38 Group) Hercules C1/C1(K)/C3 (13), transport. Codes: nil. badge: not worn.
Re-formed on 1 May 1968 at Fairford, No 30 equipped with Hercules and transferred to its present base on 24 September 1971. Principal duties are route-flying and provision of air-refuelling crews for No 1312 Flight in the Falkland Islands. Equipment is drawn from the Lyneham pool and does not bear squadron markings.

No 31 Sqn Brüggen (RAFG) Tornado GR1, strike/attack. Codes: DA-DZ. Badge: a gold star. Having been the first RAF squadron in India (December 1915), this unit led a varied career in army co-operation, transport and reconnaissance until it received strike/attack Phantoms at Brüggen in 1971. These were exchanged for Tornados on 1 November 1984, No 31 becoming the first thus equipped in the Brüggen wing.

No 32 (The Royal) Sqn Northolt (Strike/38 Group), BAe 125 CC2/CC3 (8), BAe 146 (3), Wessex HCC4 (2) and Gazelle HT3 (4), VVIP/communications. Codes: nil. Badge: not worn.
On 3 February 1969 the No 32 'number-plate' was transferred from a Canberra B15 unit at Akrotiri to the Metropolitan Communications Squadron. Responsible for carrying VIPs and non-royal VVIPs, the squadron had Andover C2s in its equipment when formed and added BAe 125s from 1971 and Gazelles from 1976. The Andovers, later including C1s and E3s converted for transport, were withdrawn from October 1993, the last in 1995, whilst all four BAe 125 CC1s were retired on 31 March 1994. The whole 125 fleet was grey by late-1993, repainting having begun in October 1988. On 1 April 1995, The Queen's Flight was moved from Benson and amalgamated with No 32 Sqn, bringing BAe 146s and Wessex. It is planned that the Gazelles will be withdrawn and replaced by civilian charter and four of the remaining 125s are to be maintained by a civilian firm.

No 33 Sqn Odiham (Strike/1 Group) Puma HC1 (12), helicopter support. Codes: CA-CZ. Badge: a hart's head in brown and buff.

Opposite:
Non-standard unit markings are worn by Wessex HCC4s of The Queen's Flight, comprising the Royal Arms between the first and second cabin windows and a Union Jack on the tailfin. *Paul Jackson*

On reformation at Odiham on 14 June 1971, the squadron equipped with Pumas, which it uses to provide tactical support for the army, including short-notice deployment overseas.

No 39 (1 PRU) Sqn Marham (Strike/1 Group), Canberra PR9 (5), T4 (2) and PR7 (2), survey and strategic reconnaissance. Codes: AA-AZ. Badge: A black winged bomb on a blue disc.
Disbanded as a Canberra PR9 Squadron on 31 May 1982, No 39 formed the basis of No 1 PRU at Wyton until this was returned to squadron status on 1 July 1992 as 'No 39 (1 PRU) Sqn'. After transferring to Marham on 30 November 1993, the squadron gained a T4 from No 360 Sqn, plus one more trainer and both remaining PR7s upon 360's disbandment in October 1994. Although assigned mostly to survey work, the PR9s began flying operational missions over Bosnia in 1993. The PR7s are used as calibration targets for the UK's air defence radar stations. No 39 is the RAF's last Canberra squadron.

No 41 Sqn Coltishall (Strike/1 Group) Jaguar GR1A (14) and T2A (2), tactical reconnaissance/battlefield air interdiction. Codes: A-Z/FA-FZ. Badge: A red Lorraine Cross surmounted by a gold crown.
Following the adoption of video reconnaissance by the Tornado GR1A, No 41's Jaguars became the only RAF tactical recce assets using 'wet film' photography until Harriers reverted to this technique in 1993. Carrying one of two types of camera pod, the squadron is assigned to the Allied Command Europe Mobile Force (Air) and has a secondary attack role. It has played a prominent role in policing operations over Northern Iraq (1991-93) and Bosnia (1993-95), the latter being the first occasion on which two-letter codes have been worn.

No 42 (Reserve) Sqn Kinloss (Strike/18 Group), Nimrod MR2 (on loan), training. Codes: nil. Badge: not worn.

A long-term maritime squadron, No 42 disbanded as a Nimrod unit at St Mawgan and was immediately re-established at Kinloss on 1 October 1992 to replace No 38 as the 'shadow' of the Nimrod OCU (until then known as No 236 OCU). It is the only squadron at Kinloss not to have its insignia applied to some aircraft of the base pool.

No 43 Sqn Leuchars (Strike/11 Group) Tornado F3 (15), air defence. Codes: GA-GZ. Badge: A fighting cock in red, yellow and blue.

The 'Fighting Cocks' have been at Leuchars since September 1969, when formed with Phantom FG1s diverted from naval contracts. Tornados began arriving in September 1989 and the squadron was declared operational on 1 July 1990.

No 45 (Reserve) Sqn No 6 FTS Finningley (P&T Command), Jetstream T1 (11), training. Codes: A-Z. Badge: A blue camel with red wings.

Disbanded on 31 March 1992 as the 'shadow' of the Tornado Weapons Conversion Unit at Honington, No 45 was re-formed at Finningley on 1 July 1992 in a non-combatant role when it became the alternative identity of the Multi-Engine Training Squadron within No 6 FTS. No 45 provides twin-conversion courses to pilots transferring from jet training to transport and maritime duties. Transfer of twin-conversion to civil training schools was announced in 1994, but the wisdom of the move is under question and the decision may be reversed.

No 47 Sqn Lyneham (Strike/38 Group) Hercules C1/C3 (13), transport. Codes: nil. Badge: not worn.

Having been the first squadron to operate the Hastings (which it flew in the Berlin Airlift) and Beverley, this unit has rightfully remained in the transport role. Re-formed with Hercules at Fairford on 25 February 1968 it moved to Lyneham on 1 February 1971, where it specialises in short-range tactical work, including carriage of special forces.

No 51 Sqn Waddington (Strike/18 Group) Nimrod R1 (3), electronic reconnaissance. Codes: nil. badge: A red and black goose.

On 21 August 1958, No 192 Sqn was renumbered at Watton, but moved to Wyton on 1 April 1963, then Waddington in 1995. Formerly equipped with Comets and Canberras, it flew its first mission with one of three new Nimrods in May 1974. The aircraft are equipped with antennae to gather details of other forces' radio/radar frequencies and procedures (the 'electronic order of battle') and have played a vital, but unsung role in the Falklands and Gulf Wars.

No 54 Sqn Coltishall (Strike/1 Group) Jaguar GR1A (14) and T2A, (2) battlefield air interdiction/close air support. Codes: GA-GZ. badge: A blue lion on a yellow shield.
No 54 is a renowned fighter squadron which re-formed with Jaguars at Lossiemouth on 29 March 1974 and was transferred to Coltishall on 8 August that year. Like the other Coltishall units (Nos 6 and 41) it is equipped to bolster the NATO flanks in wartime — in this instance classed as a Regional Reinforcement Squadron.

No 55 (Reserve) Sqn Brize Norton (Strike/38 Group) VC10, TriStar and BAe 146 (on loan), training. Codes: nil. Badge: not worn.
The last Victor tanker squadron stood-down at Marham on 1 October 1993 (formally disbanded on 15 October) and its title was immediately transferred to the former No 241 OCU at Brize Norton. Its aircraft were borrowed, as required, from Nos 10 and 101 Sqn and The Queen's Flight, but in July 1994 No 55 became a ground school only (the first numbered RAF squadron with no aircraft assigned) and the position of CO reduced from Wing Commander to Squadron Leader. The flying element of training is now handled by the aircraft operating squadrons.

No 56 (Reserve) Sqn Coningsby (Strike/11 Group) Tornado F3 (22), training. Codes: AA-AZ. Badge: A yellow Phoenix on red flames.
Disbanded at Wattisham as a Phantom FGR2 unit on 30 June 1992, this famous fighter squadron was reborn the next day, replacing No 229 OCU/No 65(R) Sqn as the Tornado F3 OCU. 'The Firebirds' are responsible for both members of the crew, pilots receiving 53hr flying in 43 sorties over 80 working days and navigators, 41hr in 31 sorties. Shorter courses are available to those with some fighter experience.

No 57 (Reserve) Sqn Lyneham (Strike/38 Group) Hercules C1/C1(K)/C3 (5), training. Codes: nil. Badge: not worn.
After disbanding as a Victor tanker squadron at Marham on 30 June 1992 No 57 returned to the order of battle when No 242 OCU was

redesignated on 1 July 1992 as 'No 57 Sqn/The Hercules OCU'. Consideration is being given to relegating No 57 to a ground school, as is already the case with No 55 Sqn.

No 60 (Reserve) Sqn Benson (Strike/1 Group) Wessex HC2 (nine), army support. Codes: A-Z. Badge: A markhor's head on a black disc.
The RAFG communications squadron disbanded at Wildenrath on 31 March 1992, having flown Andover C1/C1(PR)/CC2s. On 1 June 1992 a new Wessex squadron was established at Benson with the principal role of supporting 5 Airborne Brigade. The unit includes the Wessex Training Flight, which is an OCU for all RAF Wessex crew destined for Nos 22, 28 and 84 Sqn.

No 70 Sqn Lyneham (Strike/38 Group) Hercules C1/C3 (13), transport. Codes: nil. Badge: not worn.
Large bombers and transports have equipped this squadron for 70 years, the most recent in November 1970 when Hercules were received in Cyprus before a move to Lyneham on 15 January 1975. The main duty of No 70 is short-range tactical transport, including cargo drops by parachute-extraction.

No 72 Sqn Aldergrove (Strike/1 Group) Wessex HC2 (15), helicopter support. Codes: A-Z. Badge: A blue swallow on a red disc, flanked by blue bars.
Once a distinguished fighter squadron, No 72 re-equipped with helicopters in 1961 when Belvederes were received. The present Wessex arrived in 1964 and the squadron took up residence at Aldergrove on 12 November 1981. In October 1991, No 72 began experiments with several camouflage schemes before adopting two-tone green (later also on Pumas) early in 1992.

No 74 (Reserve) Sqn No 4 FTS Valley (P&T Command), Hawk T1/T1A, training. Codes: TA-TZ. Badge: A tiger's face.
'The Tigers' are one of the RAF's best-known

fighter squadrons, but when they disbanded as a Phantom unit on 30 September 1992, the only available means of continuation on offer was as an element of No 4 FTS. Accordingly, the unit's No 3 Training Sqn was redesignated on 1 October 1992.

No 78 Sqn Mount Pleasant (Strike/Direct reporting) Chinook HC2 (2) and Sea King HAR3 (2), helicopter support and SAR. Codes: A-Z on Chinook; (SA-SZ allocated to Sea King). Badge: A yellow lion on a black disc.
Assigned to support of the Falkland Islands garrison this unusual squadron is staffed by personnel on rotation from Europe. With only four aircraft on charge, it is the RAF's smallest unit of squadron status. It formed on 22 May 1986 from Nos 1310 (Chinook HC1) and 1564 (Sea King) Flights. The first HC2 version of Chinook was delivered by sea in February 1994. (Sea Kings wear only the first letter [S] of their codes.)

No 84 Sqn Akrotiri (Strike/Direct reporting) Wessex HC5C (4), SAR/support helicopter. Codes: nil (symbols of hearts, spades, diamonds, clubs and joker). Badge: a black scorpion.
No 84 Sqn formed at Akrotiri on 17 January 1972 with Whirlwinds and converted to Wessex HC2s in March 1982. However, in June 1984 it began receiving ex-Navy Wessex HU5s. The squadron provides local SAR cover and transports security patrols within the UK Sovereign Base Area in western Cyprus. With the phasing-out of Wessex HC2s from SAR operations in the UK, No 84 converted to this mark in November 1994 but will graduate to Sea Kings in 1999.

• **No 100 Sqn** Finningley; Leeming from late 1995; (P&T Command) Hawk T1/T1A (16), target facilities. Codes: CA-CZ. Badge: a skull on blue and yellow checkers.

This former bomber squadron, formed 11 February 1917, was established in the target facilities role on 1 February 1972, flying adapted Canberra bombers. At Wyton since 5 January 1982, it began a major change of equipment when the first replacement Hawks arrived on 5 September 1991. It recommissioned as a Hawk unit on 6 January 1992, moving to Finningley on 30 August 1993 and simultaneously transferring from Strike Command to Personnel & Training Command.

No 101 Sqn Brize Norton (Strike/38 Group) VC10 K2/K3/K4 (4/4/5), aerial refuelling. Codes: A-Z. badge: A red lion on a yellow castle, all on a black disc.
No 101 left the bomber world when re-formed on 1 May 1984 to receive tanker conversions of the VC10 airliner — most recently, on 28 April 1994, the K4. Past distinctions have included being the first operator of the Canberra (May 1951).

No 111 Sqn Leuchars (Strike/11 Group) Tornado F3 (15), air defence. Codes: HA-HZ. Badge: Three black seaxes on a yellow Palestine Cross, all on crossed red swords and a black disc.
'Treble One' has a long history of fighter operations, perpetuated since 1 May 1990 when it re-formed with Tornado F3s, to become operational on 1 January 1991 (although actually standing QRA from 13 December 1990). The unit has been at Leuchars since 3 November 1975, when it was an operator of Phantoms.

No 120 Sqn Kinloss (Strike/18 Group) Nimrod MR2 (9), maritime patrol. Codes: nil. Marking: Yellow 'CXX' on a green rectangle (on representative aircraft only).
Associated with maritime operations since 1941, No 120 moved to Kinloss with Shackletons on 1 April 1959 and began receiving Nimrods in September 1970, using the MR1 version for some 10 years. Aircraft are pooled with Nos 42(R), 120 and 206 Sqn and the squadron badges applied at Kinloss from early-1992 are only representative.

No 201 Sqn Kinloss (Strike/18 Group) Nimrod MR2 (9), maritime patrol. Codes: nil. Badge: A blue seagull (on representative aircraft only).
No 1 Sqn of the Royal Naval Air Service was renumbered No 201 Sqn on formation of the RAF on 1 April 1918. Its maritime associations continue to this day — specifically at Kinloss since 14 March 1965. Shackletons were exchanged for Nimrod MR1s from June 1970 onwards and the squadron accepted the RAF's first MR2 conversion on 23 August 1979.

No 202 Sqn (Strike/18 Group) Sea King HAR3, SAR. Codes: nil. Badge: a mallard.
Responsible for long-range, all-weather SAR around the UK coast, No 202 re-equipped from Whirlwinds to Sea Kings, beginning with its Lossiemouth detachment in August 1978. Following a division of assets associated with conversion of sister unit, No 22 Sqn to Sea Kings, its current operating locations are 'A' Flight at Boulmer; 'D' Flight at Lossiemouth; 'E' Flight at Leconfield; and the Sea King Training Unit at St Mawgan. ('B' Flight at Brawdy and 'C' Flight at Manston moved to Chivenor and Wattisham, respectively, on 1 July and 18 July 1994, simultaneously transferring to No 22 Sqn.) The HQ moved from Finningley to Boulmer on 1 December 1992. During 1992-93, the squadron's flights converted to night vision goggles, followed by the Wessex of No 22 Sqn.

No 206 Sqn Kinloss (Strike/18 Group) Nimrod MR2 (9), maritime patrol. Codes: nil. Badge: A pink octopus (on representative aircraft only).
Moving to Kinloss with Shackletons on 7 July 1965, the squadron converted to Nimrod MR1s from November 1970 and to the MR2 10 years later. Aircraft are pooled with Nos 42(R), 120 and 201 Sqn. The three operational squadrons have been providing detachments to patrol the Adriatic and enforce the Bosnian arms embargo since 1992.

No 208 (Reserve) Sqn No 4 FTS Valley (P&T Command) Hawk T1/T1A, training. Codes: DA-DZ. Marking: a yellow, winged eye.
The last Buccaneer squadron stood-down at Lossiemouth on 31 March 1994 and was reborn the following day by renumbering of No 234 Sqn at Valley. The move ended No 208's maritime connections, dating back to the days of flying boats.

No 216 Sqn Brize Norton (Strike/38 Group) TriStar K1/KC1/C2/C2A (2/4/2/1), tanker/transport. Codes: nil. Badge: a brown eagle clutching a bomb.
Despite the tanker capabilities of six of its nine TriStars, the squadron is principally involved with transporting freight and personnel. Over half its work is unscheduled support of exercises and deployments. No 216 formed in its present role on 1 November 1984 using only passenger variants. The first tanker (K1) was received on 25 March 1986; the first KC1 on 9 December 1988; first C2 on 18 September 1985 and the sole C2A on 2 April 1993.

No 230 Sqn Aldergrove (Strike/1 Group) Puma HC1 (15), helicopter support. Codes: DA-DZ. Badge: A yellow tiger's head on a black pentagon.
In October 1971, Pumas began arriving to replace Whirlwinds in No 230 Sqn. Still in the army support role, it moved from Odiham to Gütersloh on 14 October 1980 and resumed operational status in Germany on 1 December that year. Force reductions in Germany resulted in the squadron donating some of its equipment to No 18 Sqn on 30 April 1992 before relocating to Aldergrove on 4 May with an allocation of 15 helicopters to support security forces in Northern Ireland.

No 617 Sqn Lossiemouth (Strike/18 Group)
Tornado GR1B (13), maritime strike/attack.
Codes: AJ-A to AJ-Z. Marking: Red lightning flash on black ground.
'The Dam Busters' formed on 21 March 1943 and made history on 16 May that year with a raid on German dams using surface-skimming mines. The present period of operations began with re-

formation on 1 January 1983 and formal commissioning on 16 May 1983. Assigned to SACEUR's Strategic Reserve (Air) in the nuclear strike role (with co-located No 27 Sqn), the unit began training for maritime attack in 1993, with weapons including Sea Eagle anti-ship missiles. The first GR1B Tornado was received on 14 April 1994 and the squadron relocated to Lossiemouth on 27 April 1994. World War 2 code letters AJ- were 'temporarily' applied to three aircraft in 1992 for an overseas visit but soon spread to the whole squadron.

Recent disbandments

● **No 23 Sqn** disbanded as a Tornado F3 unit at Leeming on 28 February 1994.
● **No 38 (Reserve) Sqn** disbanded on 1 October 1992 at St Mawgan, having been the Nimrod OCU; replaced by No 42 (Reserve) Sqn.
● **No 63 (Reserve) Sqn** disbanded on 31 August 1992 and passed its Hawks to No 19 Sqn within No 7 FTS (No 2 TWU until 1 April 1992).
● **No 65 (Reserve) Sqn** was replaced by No 56 Sqn on 1 July 1992 as the 'shadow' of the Tornado F3 OCU (formerly No 229 OCU).
● **No 92 (Reserve) Sqn** disbanded on 30 September 1994 having been a component of No 7 FTS at Chivenor, equipped with Hawks.
● **No 115 Sqn** disbanded at Benson on 30 September 1993, passing its navaids-checking

Andovers to Hunting Aviation at East Midlands Airport.
● **No 151 (Reserve) Sqn** disbanded at Chivenor (No 7FTS, ex-No 2 TWU) on 30 August 1992 and passed its Hawks to No 92 Sqn.
● **No 234 (Reserve) Sqn** disbanded with closure of No 1 TWU at Brawdy on 31 August 1992 but re-formed at Valley on 1 November 1992 from No 2 Training Squadron of No 4 FTS — again with Hawks. It was renumbered No 208 (Reserve) Sqn on 1 April 1994.
● **No 360 Sqn** disbanded at Wyton on 31 October 1994 with Canberra T17/T17As. The unit also had two T4s and two PR7s (passed to No 39 Sqn) and flew the RAF's last Canberra B2 sortie on 7 July 1993.

FLIGHTS

When deployment of a full squadron is not demanded by circumstances, between two and four aircraft are assigned to a numbered Flight, which reports directly to Strike Command. Only two such units remain, with two Hercules and four Tornado F3s. The Tornados were delivered to the Falkland Islands on 8 July 1992, replacing Phantom FGR2s.
● **No 1312 Flight** Mount Pleasant/Hercules C1(K)/Tanker/maritime surveillance

Badge: none carried.
● **No 1435 Flight** Mount Pleasant/Tornado F3/Air defence
Marking: a Maltese Cross.

Recent disbandments

● **No 1417 Flight**, equipped with four Harrier GR3s at Belize City, stood-down on 6 July 1993.
● **No 1563 Flight**, with four Pumas at Belize City, disbanded on 31 July 1994.

OPERATIONAL CONVERSION UNITS

The role of an OCU is to convert pilots and other aircrew to a specific type of first-line aircraft and train experienced personnel as Qualified Instructors both for the OCU staff and other squadrons. In wartime, OCUs would join the order of battle with instructors flying their aircraft, either by activating their 'shadow' squadrons or splitting the OCU to reinforce two or more existing squadrons. In 1991-93 all numbered OCUs were replaced by Reserve Squadrons, details of which will be found in the listing above.

Harrier OCU	Wittering No 20(R)	Sqn (No 233 OCU until 1 September 1992)
Helicopter OCU	Odiham No 27(R)	Sqn (No 240 OCU until 1 October 1993)
Hercules OCU	Lyneham No 57(R)	Sqn (No 242 OCU until 1 July 1992)
Jaguar OCU	Lossiemouth No 16(R)	Sqn (No 226 OCU until 1 November 1991)
Nimrod OCU	Kinloss No 42(R)	Sqn (No 236 OCU until 1 October 1992)
Tornado F3 OCU	Coningsby No 56(R)	Sqn (No 229 OCU until 1 July 1992)
Transport OCU	Brize Norton No 55(R)	Sqn (No 241 OCU until 1 October 1993)
Wessex Training Flight	Benson +	

+ A component of No 60 Sqn.
Harriers of No 20(R) Sqn also wear the No 233 OCU badge of a wildcat's face.
No 55(R) Squadron includes a Tanker Training Flight.

As an intermediate stage between flying training and a fast-jet OCU, pilots previously flew 54hr on Hawks in 16 weeks at a Tactical Weapons Unit (TWU). Weapons training is now part of the FTS course, as described under Personnel & Training Command.

OTHER TRAINING UNITS

● SAR Training Unit	Wessex HC2	On loan from No 22 Sqn* Valley (Strike/18 Group)
● Sea King Training Unit	Sea King HAR3	On loan from No 202 Sqn* St Mawgan (Strike/18 Group)
● Sentry Training Squadron	Sentry AEW1	On loan from No 8 Sqn* Waddington (Strike/11 Group)
● Trinational Tornado Training Establishment	Tornado GR1/IDS	Cottesmore (Strike/1 Group) Badge: 'TTTE' within a dart, plus either a Tornado in plan ('C' Sqn) or embellished letters 'A', 'B' or 'S'.
● Tornado Weapons Conversion Unit	Tornado GR1	Lossiemouth (Strike/1 Group) See No XV (Reserve) Sqn. Badge: a crown and sword.

*Correctly, the helicopters are 'owned' by the SAR Wing at St Mawgan and the Sentries by Waddington's Engineering Wing.
TWCU aircraft wear both their own badge and the marking of No XV (Reserve) Sqn.

Recent disbandments
● **Andover Training Flight**, a component of No 32 Sqn, ceased operations in 1993.
● **Canberra Standardisation & Training Flight/No 231 OCU.** CS&TF formed at Wyton in January 1991 following disbandment of No 231 Sqn on 15 December 1990, but the OCU re-formed on 13 May 1991 and existed until disbandment on 23 April 1993.

MISCELLANEOUS UNITS

● Northolt Station Flight	Islander CC2/CC2A (1/1)	(Strike/38 Group)
● St Athan Station Flight	Hawk T1 (2)	(P&T Command)
● Strike/Attack Operational Evaluation Unit	Tornado GR1/1A (2/1), Harrier T4 (2), GR7 (4) and Jaguar T2A (1)	(Strike/AWC*) Boscombe Down
● Tornado F3 Operational Evaluation Unit	(Coningsby)	Tornado F3 (4) (Strike/AWC*)

Notes:
Northolt SF received its Islander CC2 on 17 December 1991; the CC2A followed in 1992.
* Air Warfare Centre formed at High Wycombe on 1 July 1993, incorporating Central Tactics & Trials Organisation (CTTO) at Boscombe Down, Electronic Warfare Operational Support Establishment at Wyton (later Waddington), Department of Air Warfare at Cranwell, Long-Range Maritime Patrol cell at Northwood, Operational Research Branch at High Wycombe, Support Helicopter Trials and Tactics Flight at Odiham, Rapier OEU at Honington (from April 1994) and Air Defence Ground Environment OEU at Ash. CTTO formed 30 April 1968 and its two flying units carry the badge of three swords in a 'Y' pattern: SAOEU (formed 5 October 1987 out of Tornado OEU, itself established on 1 September 1983) and F3OEU (formed 1 April 1987).

Recent disbandments
● **The Queen's Flight** was created on 1 August 1952 from The King's Flight, which had been re-established postwar on 1 May 1946. TQF was integrated in No 32 Sqn on 1 April 1995.
● **Berlin Station Flight** with two grey Chipmunk T10s disbanded at Gatow on 30 June 1994.
● **No 1 PRU** became No 39 (1 PRU) Sqn on 1 July 1992.

Recent disbandments
● **No 1 TWU** at Brawdy flew its final sortie on 27 August 1992 and disbanded on 31 August; comprised Nos 79 and 234 (Reserve) Sqn.
● **No 2 TWU** at Chivenor became No 7 FTS on 1 April 1992; comprised Nos 63 and 151 (Reserve) Sqn.

RESCUE CO-ORDINATION CENTRE

Until 1995, two RCCs — at Mount Wise, Plymouth and Pitreavie Castle, near Edinburgh — were responsible for managing SAR operations involving the RAF, Navy, Coastguard and related services. It was announced in July 1993 that Mount Wise would be disbanded in mid-1995 after Pitreavie receives new computers and communications equipment.

CONTRACTORISED UNITS

Although contractorisation is common in supporting services, the first Strike Command flying function to fall into this category was the calibration of TACAN navigation, ILS landing aids and air defence radars performed by the Andover E3s of No 115 Sqn until its disbandment at Benson on 30 September 1993. On 19 October 1993, Hunting Aviation Ltd at East Midlands Airport assumed a three-year responsibility for operating four aircraft in the same role, administered by a small Flight Checking Operations Cell at HQ No 38 Group. The Andovers retain their military serials and markings and operate anywhere in Europe. Navaids checking in the Falkland Islands is performed by Hercules C1 XV292 which is fitted with additional equipment for the role.

In 1993, FR Aviation was given the contract to replace the ECM training Canberra T17s of No 360 Sqn with eight civil-registered Dassault Falcon 20s: six at Teesside Airport and two at Bournemouth/Hurn. An interim service was available from November 1994 and the contract was fully implemented from 1 June 1995.

The first recorded charter of civil aircraft for communications flying took place in September 1994 when King Air 200 G-OAVX was leased for a short term from ATS Air Charter at Blackbushe. It retained civil markings but used an RAF call-sign.

Hunting Aviation
East Midlands   Andover E3
FR Aviation Ltd
Teesside and Hurn   Falcon 20 (civilian)

SIGNALS UNITS

Following disbandment of the intelligence-gathering No 26 SU in Berlin on 30 November 1994, most Strike Command SUs have been involved with mobile radars. These are listed in Chapter 7.

PERSONNEL & TRAINING COMMAND

On 1 April 1994, the former Support Command was divided into two: Personnel & Training Command (PTC) and Logistics Command (see later) PTC HQ is at Innsworth, where facilities were expanded in 1993 to accommodate additional staff. That said, however, the purpose of forming the two Commands was to reduce administrative manpower by 20%, and this has been achieved by merging the office of the Air Member for Personnel with the training aspects of former Support Command. PTC sets the policy and functional standards for all personnel and training within the RAF (apart from pay and allowances) and also administers legal, medical, dental and chaplaincy services. The Command also sets standards for personnel security, physical training and non-public funds. (Strike Command, similarly, takes the lead for the RAF Regiment and fire services, air traffic control and tactical communications; Logistics Command for catering, third line engineering support and health & safety at work. Commands provide these services to each other, so there is no duplication.)

The new command structure began functioning on 6 April 1994, its seven principal branches being:

● Air Secretary
● Chaplain-in-Chief
● Director of Legal Services
● Director-General of Medical Services
● Commandant Cranwell (including AOC Air Cadets)
● Commandant Bracknell (Staff College)
● Air Officer Training (including Flying Training, Ground Training, Training Support/Education and Central Flying School all headed by Air Commodores)

TRAINING GROUP DEFENCE AGENCY

As part of the new system of increased financial accountability, RAF training was re-grouped as a Defence Agency on 1 April 1994. TGDA has a staff of 6,000 military and 2,500 civilian personnel and is responsible for flying and ground activities at Chivenor, Cosford, Finningley, Halton, Hereford, Linton-on-Ouse, Locking, Newton, Scampton, Shawbury and Valley.

Flying training schools

The FTS takes prospective pilots up to 'wings' standard and provides those who will progress to fast jets with a basic course in air weaponry and tactics prior to them joining an OCU of Strike Command. Candidate pilots arrive at an FTS from one of three directions:

● **University Air Squadron**. Those intending to make a long-term career in the RAF will have received a university grant from the RAF and flown 100 or so hours on Bulldogs by the time of leaving the UAS with a Preliminary Flying Badge. Cadetships are awarded to those intending to take a Permanent Commission (to age 38) and bursaries to students who enrolled at university independently of the RAF but later decided to enter for a Short-Service Commission (12 years, plus an option on eight more).

● **Flying Scholarship**. Approximately 30hr at a civilian flying school, up to civil licence standard, paid by the RAF.

● **Direct Entry**. No previous flying experience and intending to take a short-term flying commission. Candidates are given 54hr in Fireflies of the JEFTS at Barkston Heath.

In addition, however, all will first have passed through the Officer & Aircrew Selection Centre at Cranwell (Biggin Hill until 1992) and will later have returned there (in common with all RAF officers until August 1992) of Initial Officer Training.

Following withdrawal of the Jet Provost when Course 125 graduated at Linton-on-Ouse on 4 June 1993, candidates from all three routes listed above receive basic flying training on the Tucano. Flying Scholarship trainees take the Tucano 'Long Course' of 147hr, the others, the 'Short Course' lasting 130hr (university graduates at Cranwell; direct entry at Linton-on-Ouse), the goal being fast-jet flying (known as Group 1). Students are assessed for Group 1 before the end of their course so that the last 38hr can be structured as a lead-in to the Hawk.

Pilots reckoned as unsuitable for Group 1 are moved from the Tucano course earlier. In the case of those streamed for multi-engined aircraft (Group 2), the Tucano course is 140hr (123 on the short course) the last 31hr a lead-in to the Jetstreams of the No 45 (Reserve) Sqn (otherwise known as the Multi-Engine Training Squadron) at No 6 FTS, Finningley. Here, 38hr are flown in 16 weeks on the Jetstream T1. Helicopter trainees (Group 3) leave Tucano at 63$\frac{1}{2}$hr (49$\frac{1}{2}$ 'short') for No 2 FTS and fly 88 hours in 22 weeks on Gazelles and 45 hours in 11 weeks on Wessex in 28 weeks. Those who will join a SAR squadron receive 12hr in Sea Kings and a final four Wessex hours to complete their helicopter training.

The Hawk element of training underwent a profound change in 1992-93 with introduction of the 'Mirror Image' course. Under the old system, pilots flew 75hr in 23 weeks at No 4 FTS, Valley, and then transferred to Strike Command for 54hr in 16 weeks at either No 1 or No 2 Tactical Weapons Units (TWU). This tactics and weapons training now occupies the final one-third of a slightly extended FTS course, comprising five weeks of ground school (including five simulator sorties), 65hr in 14 weeks of advanced flying and 35hr in 13 weeks using armament.

Below:
Finningley selection. Illustrating the variation in markings to be seen at one station, Tucano T1 ZF448 wears the full No 6 FTS badge flanked by blue bars; Jetstream T1 XX498 has No 45 (Reserve) Sqn's camel badge and a fin-tip marking of red diamonds on a blue band; and Bulldog T1 of Yorkshire UAS no longer wears a badge but has black and yellow rudder stripes. *Paul Jackson*

The first Mirror Image course began with No 234 Sqn of No 4 FTS on 21 September 1992, initially with the ground school. Students graduated on 3 June 1993, receiving their wings at that time and not prior to weapons training, as hitherto. It will be seen that the overall flying time has been reduced from 129hr to 100. As a result, pilots arriving at an OCU are less experienced in airmanship, so the Hawk hours 'saved' early in training have to be made up by more time on combat aircraft to achieve the same standard. This is only slightly offset by the fact that the RAF can be more choosy with its intake of students, as demand for aircrew has fallen considerably. Some Tucano graduates have to wait well over a year for a Hawk seat at an FTS. As a result of this contraction, No 7 FTS (which formed from No 2 TWU at Chivenor on 1 April 1992) was disbanded on 30 September 1994, leaving No 4 FTS as the only Hawk school.

The Central Flying School — the world's oldest flying school (formed 1912) — trains flying instructors and watches over flying standards throughout the RAF. Its courses have the same number of hours as those at the schools to which the instructors will be posted. CFS also included the Refresher Flying Flight (received from Church Fenton), where officers returning to flying after a desk-job received variable-length courses on the Jet Provost.

No 6 FTS is responsible for navigators, air engineers, air electronics officers and loadmasters. Jet Provosts were replaced here in 1993 by a combination of Tucanos and Hawks. All students begin with 15hr in Bulldogs, 30hr in Tucanos and 16.3hr in Dominies before streaming. Fast-jet selectees progress to 26hr in the Dominie and 35 in the Hawk (the final 19 Hawk hours angled either towards ground attack or air defence tactics). Multi-engine navigators receive 53.5 Dominie hours and helicopter navigators are posted to Shawbury (Gazelle/Wessex) for 50 hours of specialist instruction followed by 60 hours' flying with student helicopter pilots. The Dominie fleet has the war role of short-range maritime surveillance.

The Joint Elementary Flying Training School was established at Topcliffe in April 1993 and began operations on 8 July 1993 when Hunting Aircraft Ltd assumed the role of primary training for RAF and Royal Navy candidates. The civil-registered Slingsby T67M Mk II Fireflies replace Bulldogs of the RNEFTS previously based at Topcliffe and Chipmunks of the EFTS at Swinderby. RAF students receive 54hr and their RN compatriots, 62hr, both during a 24-week course. The unit was subordinate to No 1 FTS at Linton-on-Ouse, but moved to Barkston Heath in April 1995.

It was announced in July 1994 that all non-fast jet schools will, in future, have up to 40% civilian flying instructors. Plans for defence cost reductions include the establishment of a single helicopter basic training school for all three services, to be located either at RAF Shawbury or AAC Middle Wallop. A further economy measure will be the breaking-down of No 6 FTS and further dismemberment of CFS, relocating their components to other training stations.

● **Central Flying School** Scampton; Tucano T1 (21), Bulldog T1 (12); Marking: CFS arms; Codes: Bulldog 1-12; Chipmunk T10 (on loan); Hawk T1/T1A (11 'Red Arrows').
Det: Shawbury Gazelle HT3
Det: Valley Hawk T1/T1A (11; codes PA-PZ)
Det: SyerstonVigilant T1, Valiant T1, Viking T1 (all on loan)
● **Joint Elementary Flying Training School** Barkston Heath; Firefly (18; civil registrations)
● **No 1 FTS** Linton-on-Ouse; Tucano T1 (39); Comprising: No 1 Sqn ('A' & 'B' Flights), No 2 Sqn ('C' & 'D' Flights) and No 3 Sqn ('E' & 'F' Flights); Marking: '1 FTS' Det: Topcliffe (See JEFTS)
● **No 2 FTS** Shawbury; Gazelle HT3 (19), Wessex HC2 (10); Marking: nil; Codes: Gazelle A-Z; Wessex WA-WZ
● **No 3 FTS** Cranwell; Tucano T1 (56); Marking: blue fuselage band
● **No 4 FTS** Valley; Hawk T1 (72); Comprising: Nos 19 (R), 74 (R) and 208 (R) Sqn
● **No 6 FTS** Finningley; Basic Navigation Wing: No 1 BNTS Bulldog (five), Tucano (nine)
No 2 BNTS Dominie (11)
Ground School Squadron nil
Officer Training Squadron nil
Advanced Navigation Wing: Hawk Squadron Hawk (nine)
Air Navigation Training Squadron loaned aircraft
Navigation School Standards Squadron loaned aircraft
No 45(R) Sqn/METS Jetstream T1 (10)
Joint FAC Standards & Training Unit Hawk on loan
Markings: RAF Finningley badge (plus blue rudder on Bulldogs; No 45 Sqn winged camel on Jetstreams); Codes: Bulldog V-Z; Dominie A-Z; Jetstream A-L

Ground training units

Limited space precludes a complete listing of non-flying units engaged in instruction. However, a number of these have static training airframes visible within their grounds or accessible on open days.

● **No 1 School of Technical Training**, Cosford. Opened 4 August 1938 as No 2 SofTT; last apprentice course (No 155) graduated 7 October 1993; redesignated No 1 SofTT, early-1995, offering multi-skill courses.
● **No 4 School of Technical Training** St Athan. Approximately eight airframes for civilian craft training.
● **Servicing Instruction Flight**, Cranwell.

Approximately eight Hunters in taxiable condition. Badge: An owl with mortar board and cane flanked by red/white/red bars.
● **Trade Management Training School**, Scampton. Approximately eight Hunters in taxiable condition.

Other significant instructional establishments are:
● **Bracknell** RAF Staff College (to close in 1997)
● **Halton** General Service Training wing (comprising School of Recruit Training and Airmen's Command School); Guided Weapons School and School of Education
● **Henlow** Civilian Technical Training School
● **Locking** No 1 Radio School
● **Newton** RAF Police Dog Training Squadron (to close)
● **Shawbury** Central Air Traffic Control School
● **Wyton** Joint School of Photographic Interpretation

Notes:
At No 1 SofTT, Halton, the final apprentice course (No 155) graduated on 24 June 1993 and transfer began of engineering trade training facilities to Cosford where the unit reopened in early-1995, replacing No 2 SofTT. Before transfer to Halton the School of Recruit Training graduated its final course at Swinderby on 16 July 1993. The first graduation at Halton after an eight-week course was on 18 January 1994. Newton's airfield closed in July 1994 and the Guided Weapons School, Police School and School of Education moved to Halton, leaving an RAF enclave from March 1995 onwards. Hereford, previous home of the Airmen's Command School, closed in July 1994.

OTHER UNITS

Outside the Training Group Defence Agency are the air cadet and university units and some miscellaneous formations.

University Air Squadrons
Administered since 1971 by HQ UAS at Cranwell, UASs date back to October 1925 when units were formed at Oxford and Cambridge. London UAS was established in 1935 and 21 more in 1941. Consolidation has taken place, and some UASs renamed to allow for an expanded catchment. Replacement of Chipmunks by Bulldogs began in September 1973 and ended in March 1975. One non-standard unit is the RAF College Air Squadron which was formed as recently as 1992 for students at Cranwell. UASs are components of the RAuxAF and their few permanent RAF staff are assisted by members of the RAF Volunteer Reserve. They provide 30% of the RAF's pilot intake, including half of the fast-jet pilots.

Bristol UAS moved from Filton to Hullavington, then to Colerne early in 1993; Southampton UAS from Lee-on-the-Solent to Boscombe Down on

2 April 1993; and Queens UAS from Sydenham to Aldergrove in 1992.

● **Aberdeen, Dundee & St Andrews UAS** Leuchars; Bulldog T1 (4); Badge: lion holding a tower; Codes: A-E
● **Birmingham UAS** Cosford; Bulldog T1 (6); Badge: a double-headed lion; also Aston, Coventry, Keele, Staffordshire, Warwick and Wolverhampton; Codes: A-F
● **Bristol UAS** Colerne; Bulldog T1 (5); Badge: a galleon; also Bath; Codes: A-F
● **Cambridge UAS** Cambridge; Bulldog T1 (4); Badge: a lion; also E Anglia and Essex; Codes: C,U,A,S
● **East Lowlands UAS** Edinburgh; Bulldog T1 (4); Badge: open book and white cross; also Heriot-Watt, Napier College and Stirling; Codes: 01-04
● **East Midlands UAS** Newton; Bulldog T1 (6); Badge: a quiver of arrows; also Leicester; Codes: E,M,U,A,S,'π'
● **Glasgow & Strathclyde UAS** Glasgow; Bulldog T1 (5); Badge: a dove and sword; also Paisley; Codes: A-Z
● **Liverpool UAS** Woodvale; Bulldog T1 (4); Badge: a cormorant and book; also Lancaster, John Moores and Central Lancashire; Codes: L,U,A,S
● **London UAS** Benson; Bulldog T1 (5); Badge: a globe and open book; Codes: 1-10
● **Manchester UAS** Woodvale; Bulldog T1 (6); Badge: a sparrowhawk and snake; also Salford; Codes: 1-6
● **Northumbrian UAS** Leeming; Bulldog T1 (6); Badge: a white cross; Durham and Newcastle; Codes: U-Z
● **Oxford UAS** Benson; Bulldog T1 (4); Badge: open book and crossed sword and staff; Codes: A-D
● **Queens UAS** Aldergrove; Bulldog T1 (4); Badge: a winged torch; also N Ireland Poly and New University; Codes: A-E
● **Southampton UAS** Boscombe Down; Bulldog T1 (7); Badge: a stag and pillar; also Portsmouth Poly; Codes: 01-07
● **U Wales AS** St Athan; Bulldog T1 (7); Badge: dragon and open book; also Glamorgan; Codes: 01-07
● **Yorkshire UAS** Finningley; Bulldog T1 (8) Marking: black/yellow rudder; Bradford, Hull, Leeds, Sheffield and York; Codes: A-H
● **RAF College Air Sqn** Cranwell; Bulldog T1 (6); Marking: blue/white/red rudder; Codes: A1, A2, B1, B2, C1, C2

HEADQUARTERS AIR CADETS

Situated at Newton and commanded by an Air Commodore, HQAC administers the Air Training Corps and provides support to the 185 RAF sections of the Combined Cadet Corps, which is organised on a school basis. There are currently 40,000 cadets aged between 13 and 20 in 925 squadrons and 97 detached flights of this voluntary organisation, from which the RAF receives some 35% of all its regular entrants, and 50% of officers. The ATC is the world's largest glider training organisation, but cadets also fly regularly in Chipmunks. Additionally, the Corps allocates annually over 300 Flying Scholarships (30 flying hours at a civilian school), 50 navigation scholarships (10hr), 800 flightdeck flights on civil airliners and other aircraft and 70 RAF overseas flights. The ATC operates 57 Chipmunks, one Bulldog, 53 Vigilant T1 power-assisted sailplanes, 95 Viking T1s, four Valiant T1s and two Janus Cs. *Notes:*

VOLUNTEER GLIDING SCHOOLS

There are two types of VGS: self-launching (Vigilant T1) and winch-launching. Following replacement of the Slingsby T21 and T31, schools have operated one type of sailplane only, although a recent departure has been allocation of a few remaining Valiants to augment selected units, these having been held by the Air Cadets' Central Gliding School until 1992. ACCGS operates both Janus Cs, although these may be flown from locations other than Syerston. The first two digits of the VGS number refer to the long-defunct Nos 61-64 and 66 Groups of RAF Home Command in which particular schools were located. Survivors of the original schools, numbered 1 GS-203 GS, were renumbered in this system in 1955 and those formed subsequently have followed its regional plan. The ATC is now divided into seven home regions:

● Central & East Region	(ex part of No 61 Group)
● London & South-East Region	(ex part of No 61 Group)
● South-West Region	(ex No 62 Group)
● Welsh Region	(ex part of No 63 Group)
● North-West Region	(ex part of No 63 Group)
● North-East Region	(ex No 64 Group)
● Scotland & Northern Ireland Region	(ex No 66 Group)

● No 611 VGS	Swanton Morley	Viking T1 (6)
● No 612 VGS	Halton	Vigilant T1 (2)
● No 613 VGS	Halton	Vigilant T1 (4)
● No 614 VGS	Wethersfield	Viking T1 (4)
● No 615 VGS	Kenley	Viking T1 (8)
● No 616 VGS	Henlow	Vigilant T1 (4)
● No 617 VGS	Manston	Viking T1 (3)
● No 618 VGS	West Malling	Viking T1 (7), Valiant T1 (1)
● No 621 VGS	Hullavington	Viking T1 (4)
● No 622 VGS	Upavon	Viking T1 (6), Valiant T1 (1)
● No 624 VGS	Chivenor	Vigilant T1 (3)
● No 625 VGS	Hullavington	Viking T1 (5)
● No 626 VGS	Predannack	Viking T1 (3)
● No 631 VGS	Sealand	Viking T1 (8)
● No 632 VGS	Ternhill	Vigilant T1 (5)
● No 633 VGS	Cosford	Vigilant T1 (5)
● No 634 VGS	St Athan	Viking T1 (4)
● No 635 VGS	Samlesbury	Vigilant T1 (4)
● No 636 VGS	Swansea	Viking T1 (3)
● No 637 VGS	Little Rissington	Viking T1 (4)
● No 642 VGS	Linton-on-Ouse	Vigilant T1 (5)
● No 644 VGS	Syerston	shares aircraft of ACCGS
● No 645 VGS	Catterick	Viking T1 (5)
● No 661 VGS	Kirknewton	Viking T1 (4)
● No 662 VGS	Arbroath	Viking T1 (5), Valiant T1 (1)
● No 663 VGS	Kinloss	Vigilant T1 (3)
● ACCGS	Syerston	Vigilant T1 (14), Viking T1 (12), Valiant T1 (1), Janus C (2)
● CGMF	Syerston	(Central Glider Maintenance Facility)

Recent changes have included transfer of No 612 VGS from Benson, No 621 from Weston-super-Mare and No 625 from South Cerney. No 643 VGS disbanded at Binbrook and No 664 has not been re-formed following a 'temporary' stand-down in 1990.

All units have devised unofficial badges, but none is applied to an aircraft. No codes are applied.

AIR EXPERIENCE FLIGHTS

Chipmunks are assigned to each of 12 AEFs, the other having a single Bulldog (which is included in Queen's UAS strength). All AEFs were formed in mid-1958. Some aircraft carry unofficial badges. There appears to be a national number-code system for AEFs, but only six units comply.

● **No 1 AEF**	Manston	Chipmunk T10 (4)	Codes: 3-6	
● **No 2 AEF**	Hurn	Chipmunk T10 (4)	Codes: 9-12	
● **No 3 AEF**	Colerne	Chipmunk T10 (8)	Codes: A-Z	
● **No 4 AEF**	Exeter	Chipmunk T10 (4)	Codes: A-Z	
● **No 5 AEF**	Teversham	Chipmunk T10 (8)	Codes: A-Z	Marking: a winged 'V'
● **No 6 AEF**	Benson	Chipmunk T10 (8)	Codes: A-Z	Marking: Uffington white horse
● **No 7 AEF**	Newton	Chipmunk T10 (4)	Codes: 71-75	Marking: Robin Hood with '7'
● **No 8 AEF**	Shawbury	Chipmunk T10 (4)	Codes: 8, A, E, F	
● **No 9 AEF**	Finningley	Chipmunk T10 (4)	Codes: 67-69	
● **No 10 AEF**	Woodvale	Chipmunk T10 (4)	Codes: 91-95	Marking: a red rose
● **No 11 AEF**	Leeming	Chipmunk T10 (4)	Codes: 83-86	Marking: a winged '11'
● **No 12 AEF**	Turnhouse	Chipmunk T10 (1)	Codes: nil	
● **No 13 AEF**	Aldergrove	Bulldog T1 (1)	Codes: nil	

Notes:
No 3 AEF moved from Bristol/Filton to Hullavington, then to Colerne in 1992-93; No 13 AEF from Sydenham to Aldergrove in 1992.

MISCELLANEOUS FLYING UNITS

The Battle of Britain Memorial Flight (formed July 1957) expanded during 1993 with the addition of a Dakota. The RAF Institute of Aviation Medicine at Farnborough (formed 11 September 1950) possessed two Hawks but on 1 April 1994 the unit began a two-year programme of incorporation within the Defence Research Agency's Centre for Human Factors. The Hawks are now based at Boscombe Down on DRA charge and the former IAM laboratories at Farnborough remain in use (and will gain a new centrifuge in 1996), but also under the DRA-CHF banner despite a continued RAF administrative presence.

● **BBMF**   Coningsby: Lancaster BI, Spitfire IIA/VB/PRXIX, Hurricane IIC, Devon C2, Dakota C4, Chipmunk T10

LOGISTICS COMMAND

One of the two Commands formed on 1 April 1994 from the former Support Command, Logistics Command is responsible for maintenance, storage and distribution. Its HQ is at Brampton, with associated Wytpn from 1 April 1995. Main components of the new Command are the facilities once assigned to the Air Officer Commanding Maintenance Units at Support Command and the office of the Air Member for Supply and Organisation from MoD London. The officer commanding continues to have the dual title of AMSO and AOC-in-C Logistics Command.

Logistics Command, with a staff of 20,850, brings together the Maintenance Group Defence Agency (formed 1 April 1991 as a self-managing agency responsible for third-line repair and overhaul, depot storage and now, some signals units); Support Management Group (from London, High Wycombe and Harrogate); and the newly-formed Logistics Support Services organisation (comprising Supply Control Division at Stanbridge; and Centralised Servicing Development Establishment and Maintenance Analysis & Computing Division, both at Swanton Morley, but to transfer to Wyton). Other self-managing agencies later added to the organisation have been the RAF Signals Engineering Establishment at Henlow on 22 November 1994 and Defence Helicopter Support Agency (for all the UK's 800 military

Opposite:
Larger then life. A non-standard unit badge (compare aircraft behind) was applied by No 74(R) Sqn to Hawk T1 XX226 which had been painted all-black for conspicuity trials in 1992. *Paul Jackson*

helicopters) at Yeovilton on 1 April 1994. The four main offices of Logistics Command are:
● COS/Air Officer Strategic Policy and Plans (directly-administered units)
● Director-General Support Management
● AOM/AOC Maintenance Units
● AOCIS/AOC Signals Units

Maintenance units

The old, numbered MUs have mostly disappeared with the transfer of much aircraft engineering work to St Athan. However, civil firms are increasingly being contracted to undertake work which would formerly have taken place at an MU, most notably aircraft painting and the RAF Exhibition Flight of genuine and plastic display airframes which is managed by SERCO Ltd. A new 'MU' formed within the Royal Navy Armament Depot at Crombie, near Edinburgh, on 1 April 1994, when the Integrated Weapon Complex opened to maintain Sea Eagle and Alarm missiles previously serviced by STCASMSU at Marham and Alarm Maintenance Facility at Cottesmore.

Major locations

● **St Athan** Principal aircraft overhaul facility. Includes Aircraft Engineering Wing (Nos 1, 2, 3, 4 and 10 Sqn), General Engineering Wing (Nos 5, 6, 7 and 8 Sqn) and Engineering Plans & Development Wing (No 9 Sqn); Repair & Salvage Squadron. At any one time, St Athan will have some 68 aircraft undergoing overhaul, typically 32 Tornados, 10 Harriers/Sea Harriers, 14 Hawks, seven Jaguars, two VC10s, one Jetstream, one Dominie and one Spitfire.
● **Shawbury** No 27 MU has increased its activities in recent years and by late-1994 had 102 aircraft in storage, most notably 33 Tucanos (with more possibly to follow). In addition to Bulldogs, Chipmunks, Harriers and Jaguars are non-effective types: Jet Provost (14) and Phantom FGR2 (six).

Secondary locations

● **Cardington** No 217 MU (compressed gas production)
● **Carlisle** No 14 MU (general storage); to close 31 March 1997; stocks to No 16 MU
● **Crombie** Integrated Weapon Complex (Sea Eagle and Alarm)
● **Hartlebury** No 25 MU (general storage)
● **Hullavington** Parachute Servicing Flight
● **Kingswinford** Exhibition Flight (recruiting display airframes at civilian location)
● **North Luffenham** Ground Radio Servicing Centre; Electronics Battle Damage Repair & Prevention Development Centre; to close 30 September 1996; residents to No 30 MU.
● **Quedgeley** No 7 MU (general and tri-service domestic equipment); to close 31 March 1998; stocks to No 16 MU
● **Sealand** No 30 MU (avionics repair)
● **Stafford** No 16 MU (general storage)

● **Wyton** Centralised Servicing Development Establishment

Notes:
No 11 MU at Chilmark, the bomb storage unit, was closed on 27 January 1995 and Swanton Morley followed later in the year when the CSDE moved to Wyton.

SIGNALS UNITS
Listed in Chapter 7.

DIRECTLY-ADMINISTERED UNITS
These include the much-maligned but excellent catering services; the RAF Mountain Rescue Service (formed 22 January 1944) with teams at Kinloss, Leuchars, Leeming, St Athan, Stafford and Valley; and RAF Music Services at Uxbridge (which is also, since 1 April 1994, parent station for RAF staff at West Drayton air traffic control centre). RAF Stanbridge is the Supply Control Centre (the co-located Joint Services Air Trooping Centre closed in 1995). The last RAF hospital in the UK, at Wroughton, will close in 1997.

RAF GLIDING AND SOARING ASSOCIATION AND RAF MICROLIGHT FLYING ASSOCIATION

Formed on 15 December 1949, the RAFGSA is independent of the Ministry of Defence, although it does receive financial help from the RAF Sports Board and the Nuffield Trust, and is able to use military airfields for its weekend activities. Its aim is to 'bring gliding and soaring within the reach of all members of the RAF, with special regard to those employed on the ground.' Equipment is serialled in the range RAFGSA1 to RAFGSA99 with reuse of numbers when old aircraft are withdrawn. Powered tugs (eg, Chipmunks and Pawnee) are on the UK civil register. The following gliding clubs are based in the UK:

● **RAFGSA Centre**	Bicester
● **Anglia GC**	Wattisham
● **Bannerdown GC**	Hullavington
● **Chilterns GC**	Halton
● **Clevelands GC**	Dishforth
● **Cranwell GC**	Cranwell North
● **Four Counties GC**	Syerston
● **Fenland GC**	Marham
● **Fulmar GC**	Kinloss
● **Humber GC**	Scampton
● **Wrekin GC**	Cosford

Bases abroad with RAFGSA sailplanes are:
● **Brüggen** (Germany)
● **Kingsfield** (Cyprus)
● **Laarbruch** (Germany)

Somewhat newer, the RAFMA received its first aircraft, a Solar Wings Quantum 15, at Halton in January 1994. However, the Association had previously sponsored training at the Ridgerunners Flying Centre — a privately-funded group run by military personnel at Halton. It is planned to run training camps throughout the UK in addition to courses at Halton. Aircraft are on the UK microlight register.

3 Aircraft and missiles

With the passage of time, aircraft are redesigned to adopt different roles, modified to take on secondary tasks or rebuilt to do their work more efficiently. Such changes are normally accompanied by a variation of their mark number. With a few exceptions, aircraft receive a name in addition to the manufacturer's designation, the first variant of which is, logically enough, Mark 1. This is prefixed by letter or letters to indicate the aircraft's function, for example Tornado GR Mk 1 — usually written as GR1. Minor modifications to the original GR (Ground attack and Reconnaissance) capability produce the GR1A and GR1B, but a major redesign as an air superiority fighter yields the F2. With upgraded engines and avionics, this has become the F3, whilst the GR4 is shortly to appear through modification of GR1 airframes with the latest operational equipment.

Suffixes denote secondary roles or addition of special equipment. For example, the VC10 C1(K) is a transport (C) having tanker (K) capability which either does not interfere with the primary role or can be easily removed. Close study of designations will reveal some exceptions and inconsistencies (such as the BAe 125 and Dominie being regarded as unrelated aircraft), but the above is sufficient to outline the practice. Role prefixes and suffixes in current use with the RAF and some research units are as below.

been so modified, the differentiation is superfluous.

The designation Tornado GR1(T) and F3(T) for aircraft with dual control is occasionally seen, but is not official. All are fully combat-capable.

PRINCIPAL AIRCRAFT TYPES

This guide does not seek to duplicate basic specifications quoted in guides such as Ian Allan's *abc Combat Aircraft Recognition*. In the following pages, salient points are indicated for general interest or as a guide to further study.

Where applicable, manufacturers' names are those in use at the time at which the final aircraft was built.

Prefixes:

● AEW	Airborne Early Warning
● C	Cargo (Transport)
● D	Drone (formerly U — unmanned)
● CC	Communications (ie VIP)
● E	Electronic (calibration)
● F	Fighter
● GR	Ground attack & Reconnaissance
● HAR	Helicopter, Air Rescue
● HC	Helicopter, Cargo
● HCC	Helicopter, Communications (ie VIP)
● HT	Helicopter, Trainer
● K	Tanker
● KC	Tanker & Cargo (transport)
● MR	Maritime Reconnaissance
● PR	Photographic Reconnaissance
● R	Reconnaissance (ELINT)
● T	Trainer
● W	Weather (research)

Suffixes:

● K	Tanker
● P	Refuelling probe
● PR	Photographic Reconnaissance

Notes:
Some Hercules and Nimrods received (P) after their designation to denote addition of refuelling probes. Now that all aircraft of this type have

Below:
Harrier GR7 cockpit.

Top:

Boeing Helicopters Chinook HC2

Medium-lift helicopter; Nos 7, 18, 27 and 78 Sqn. **1** Forward antenna for Marconi ARI 18228 radar warning receiver; **2** crew door (loadmaster observing lifting operation) and optional position for 7.62mm machine-gun; **3** forward cargo hook — maximum 17,000lb; **4** main cargo hook — maximum 26,000lb; **5** rear cargo hook — maximum 17,000lb (total maximum load 26,000lb); **6** chaff dispenser; **7** steerable rear wheel; **8** rear loading ramp; **9** provision for AN/ALQ-157 infra-red jammer; **10** flare dispenser; **11** rear antenna for ARI 18228; **12** rear sensor for AN/AAR-47 missile approach warner; **13** Lycoming T55-L-712F turboshafts (total two); **14** provision for two-man hoist; **15** forward sensors for AN/AAR-47; **16** pilot and co-pilot (cockpit optimised for night-vision goggles); *Notes:* Total 41 HC1s received; surviving 32 being upgraded by Boeing in USA to HC2 by mid-1995 (last Mk 1 left UK in July 1994); three new HC2s for delivery late in 1995.

Above:

British Aerospace/McDonnell Douglas Harrier GR7

Short Take-Off/Vertical Landing (STO/VL) battlefield air interdiction and close air support;

Nos 1, 3 and IV and 20 (Reserve) Sqn and SAOEU. **1** Hughes Angle Rate Bombing Set (ARBS) sensor window; **2** GEC forward-looking infra-red (FLIR); **3** wind direction sensor (simple weathercock); **4** one-man cockpit (raised and modernised, compared with GR3); **5** Rolls-Royce Pegasus Mk 105 vectored-thrust turbofan; **6** front (cold) zero-scarf (non cut away) nozzle; **7** inner wing pylon — max 2,000lb; **8** Sidewinder AAM pylon, with built-in Bofors BOL 304 chaff dispenser; **9** mid-wing pylon — max 2,000lb; **10** outer wing pylon — max 620lb (total permissible weapon load 13,325lb, including 2,000lb on fuselage centreline); **11** Marconi ARI 23333 Zeus electronic countermeasures suite forward high-band receiver; **12** Zeus low-band receiver; **13** Zeus rear high-band receiver; **14** retracted outrigger wheel; **15** Plessey missile approach warning radar; **16** Zeus jamming transmitter; **17** Zeus low-band receiver; **18** flush antenna for Global Positioning System;

Notes: Total 96 ordered; last 34 as GR7, others upgraded from GR5/5A; final new delivery in June 1992; last conversion in 1995; 90 remain in service. Delivery in progress of 13 two-seat Harrier T10s to replace first-generation T4/T4As (28 built). *RAF*

British Aerospace Hawk T1/T1A
Advanced flying trainer and basic weapons trainer and target-tug; No 4 FTS, No 6 FTS, CFS, Red Arrows, No 100 and Nos 19, 74 and 208 (Reserve) Sqn. **1** pitot tube; **2** provision for ADEN 30mm cannon pod on centreline; **3** optional pylon for BGT AIM-9L Sidewinder AAM; **4** new all-black colour scheme for daytime high-visibility; **5** Rolls-Royce/Turbomeca Adour Mk 151 turbofan; **6** raised rear cockpit for instructor; **7** single-piece canopy, hinged on starboard side; **8** Ferranti F195 gunsight. *Notes:* Items 2, 3 and 8 omitted on aircraft assigned to basic and (No 6 FTS) navigator training; fleet being re-winged, modified aircraft having provision for one pylon each side, designated T1W. Total 176 ordered; 89 converted to T1A; 146 remain (including transfers to Royal Navy and trials aircraft).

Lockheed C-130K Hercules C3
Tactical transport; Nos 24, 30, 47, and 70 Sqn, No 1312 Flight and No 57 (Reserve) Sqn/Hercules OCU. **1** Four-crew cockpit; **2** refuelling probe; **3** Allison T55-A-15 turboprop engines (total four); **4** Lockheed Sanders AN/ALR-66 radar warning receivers in wingtips; **5** rear loading ramp (and aperture for refuelling hose of tanker version); **6** 1,132gal external fuel tanks; **7** belly radome for AN/APN-169B station-keeping equipment; **8** cargo hold for 92 paratroops or 38,900lb of freight (64 or 42,670lb in Hercules C1); **9** Ekco E290 radar.
Notes: Hercules C1(K) is tanker version; C3 fuselage 'stretched' by 15ft; W2 is one-off research aircraft for DERA Meteorological Research Flight. War zone defensive measures optional fit includes AN/ALQ-157 infra-red jammers and AN/ALE-40 flare dispensers; five with Racal 'Orange Blossom' wingtip ESM pods. Total 66 bought; five lost; five for sale in 1995.
RAF

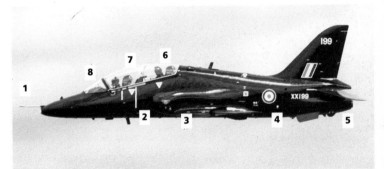

Above:
SEPECAT Jaguar GR1A
Attack and reconnaissance fighter; Nos 6, 41 and 54 and No 16 (Reserve) Sqn and SAOEU; **1** Ferranti LRMTS (Laser Ranger and Marked Target Seeker); **2** single-seat cockpit; **3** light grey medium-level camouflage for operations over Bosnia; **4** Marconi ARI 18223 radar warning receiver; **5** over-wing BGT AIM-9L Sidewinder AAMs; **6** Rolls-Royce/Turbomeca Adour Mk 104 reheated turbofan (total two); **7** 1,000lb Mk 22 bomb; **8** 264gal drop-tanks; **9** ADEN 30mm cannon; **10** Philips-MATRA Phimat chaff dispenser pod (Westinghouse AN/ALQ-101(V)-10 jammer on port side); **11** Tracor AN/ALE-40 flare dispensers beneath engines; **12** retracted refuelling probe.
Notes: T2A is two-seat trainer with operational capability; GR1B (10 conversions) and T2B (two) carry TIALD laser designator pads. Total 165/38 single/two-seat Jaguars built; 66/22 remain.

Below:
British Aerospace Nimrod MR2
Maritime reconnaissance; Nos 120, 201 and 206 and No 38 (Reserve) Sqn. ELINT; No 51 Sqn. **1** Thorn EMI ARI 5980 Searchwater radar; **2** weapons bay; **3** Rolls-Royce RB168-20 Spey turbofan (total four); **4** sonobuoy chutes; **5** rear-facing launcher for marker flares; **6** aerodynamic compensating fin for nose-probe; **7** MAD boom; **8** aerodynamic compensating fins for wingtip pods; **9** Loral EW-1017 (ARI 18240/1) 'Yellow Gate' ESM pods; **10** searchlight (starboard side only); **11** eight or more tactical crew in cabin; **12** refuelling probe; **13** three flightdeck crew.
Notes: Nimrod R1 has no MAD boom and additional aerials at several points. Special war zone fit is two Bofors BOZ 107 chaff/flare pods on underwing pylons; FLIR turret under starboard wing; and AN/AAR-47 missile approach warners in wing pods and at base of MAD boom. Total 48 MR1 and three R1 built; 28 MR2s operational, plus four in long-term storage; three R1s remain.

Top:

Westland/Aerospatiale SA330E Puma HC1

Support helicopter; Nos 27 (Reserve), 33 and 230 Sqn. **1** Forward antenna for Marconi ARI 18228 radar warning receiver; **2** 'Polyvalent' air filters; **3** Turbomeca Turmo IIIC4 turboshaft (total two); **4** composites material rotor blade; **5** rear ARI 18228; **6** provision for two Tracor M130 chaff/flare dispensers; **7** starboard rear sensor for Honeywell AN/AAR-47 missile approach warner; **8** retractable undercarriage; **9** sliding door to cabin and optional position for 7.62mm machine-gun; **10** cargo hook; **11** pilot and navigator; **12** forward starboard AN/AAR-47.

Notes: Puma Navigation Update (PNU) avionics improvement programme launched February 1993 for completion in 1996. Total 49 bought; 42 remain.

Above:

Westland/Sikorsky Sea King HAR3/3A

SAR helicopter; Nos 22, 78 and 202 Sqn and SKTU. **1** No 202 Sqn badge; **2** retractable undercarriage; **3** cargo hook; **4** sponson for buoyancy on water; **5** sliding cabin door; **6** boat hull; **7** break-line of folding tail; **8** MEL ARI 5955 radar; **9** two-man winch; **10** Rolls-Royce Gnome H1400-1 turboshaft (total two); **11** two pilots (radar operator and winchman in cabin) equipped with night-vision goggles from 1992.

Notes: No 78 Sqn aircraft fitted with ARI 18228 radar warning receivers. Total 19 built; six more on order, designated HAR3A, to be delivered from 1995 with revised avionics including ARI 5955/2 radar.

Below:
Boeing E-3D Sentry AEW1
Airborne early warning; No 8 Sqn and STS. **1** Bendix-King weather radar; **2** four flightdeck crew; **3** exhaust for auxiliary power unit; **4** HF radio antenna on wing trailing edge; **5** Loral EW-1017 (ARI 18240/1) 'Yellow Gate' ESM pod; **6** Westinghouse AN/APY-2 radar rotodome; **7** CFM International CFM56-2A turbofan (total four); **8** 13-person tactical crew; **9** No 8 Sqn 'fighter bars' astride roundel; **10** receptacle for USAF-style 'flying boom' refuelling; **11** probe for RAF-style drogue refuelling.
Notes: Wingtip pods only on RAF E-3s. Total seven aircraft.

Bottom:
Panavia Tornado GR1/1A/1B
Strike/attack, plus (GR1A) reconnaissance and (GR1B) anti-shipping attack; Nos II, IX, 12, 13, 14, 17, 31 and 617 Sqn, TTTE, TWCU/No 45 (Reserve) Sqn and SAOEU. **1** Texas Instruments radar and terrain-following radar; **2** pilot's seat; **3** navigator's seat (some aircraft have minimal-standard dual control added); **4** port forward antenna for Marconi Hermes radar homing and warning receiver; **5** Turbo Union RB199 Mk 103 reheated turbofans (total two); **6** rear Hermes antenna and No 12 Sqn markings; **7** Bofors BOZ 103 chaff/flare pod (GEC-Marconi Sky Shadow jamming pod on port side); **8** 330gal drop-tank (495gal tank optional, but reduces maximum wing-sweep from 67° to 63°); **9** launch rail for BGT AIM-9L Sidewinder self-defence AAM; **10** position for under-fuselage sensor on GR1A; **11** position of side windows (port and starboard) on GR1A; **12** Ferranti LRMTS (Laser-Ranger and Marked Target Seeker); **13** IWKA-Mauser 27mm cannon (total two) (not on GR1A).
Notes: Total 219 production aircraft; 30 built as/converted to GR1A; 24 converted to GR1B (illustrated); 142 to be converted to GR4 with upgraded avionics; 181 of all versions remain in service.

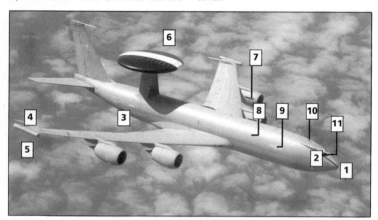

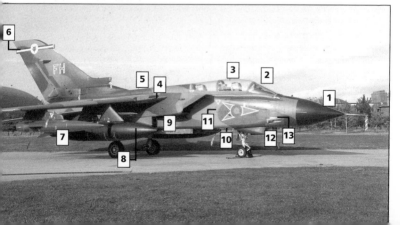

Top:
Panavia Tornado F3
Air defence; Nos 11, 25, 29, 43 and 111 Sqn, plus Tornado F3 OCU/No 56 (Reserve) Sqn and ADOEU (F3OEU). **1** Marconi AI 24 'Foxhunter' radar; **2** semi-recessed stowage for four BAe Sky Flash AAMs; **3** variable geometry wings, sweeping between 25° and 67°; **4** Turbo Union RB199 Mk 104 reheated turbofans; **5** all-moving stabilator; **6** extended reheat pipe of Mk 104 engine; **7** leading-edge slats extended for improved low-speed handling; **8** pylons for BGT AIM-9L Sidewinder AAMs (inner and outer sides of pylon); **9** checkered fighter bars of No 43 Sqn; **10** pilot and navigator.
Notes: Two Tornado F2s in trials use; 16 to be used for F3 rebuilds. Total 170 production aircraft, including 18 F2s; 165 remain, but 24 to be leased to Italy.

Above:
Lockheed 1011 TriStar K1/KC1/C2/C2A
Tanker (K1), tanker-transport (KC1) and, as illustrated, passenger transport (C2/C2A); No 216 Sqn. **1** position for refuelling probe (removed from KC1; not fitted to C2/C2A); **2** four flight deck crew; **3** 267 passenger seats (K1 has freight space forward and 187 seats at rear; KC1 variable between up to 266 seats and all-freight); **4** Rolls-Royce RB211-524B turbofan (two under wings); **5** air duct for third RB211; **6** No 216 Sqn badge; **7** leading-edge slats extended for landing; **8** two FRL Mk 17T hose-and-drum units in lower rear fuselage; **9** four-wheel main undercarriage bogies; **10** K1/KC1 only: under-floor tanks for extra 12,830gal of fuel, increasing total to 38,885gal.
Notes: Mk 2s have normal tankage, including C2A with military-standard communications and navigation equipment. Total two K1s, four KC1s two C2s and one C2A.

Above:

BAC VC10 C1(K)/K2/K3/K4

Tanker and C1(K) tanker/transport; Nos 10 and 101 Sqn. **1** Four-man flightdeck; **2** cabin — 150 passengers in C1(K), but up to 17 only in tanker versions, with remainder occupied by extra tanks for 3,500gal of fuel, total capacity 20,737gal in K2 and 22,609gal in K3, but C1K and K4 have only standard fuel capacity of Super VC10; **3** badge of No 101 Sqn; **4** forward antennae for GEC-Marconi ARI 18223/17 Sky Guardian radar warning receiver in fin 'bullet'; **5** exhaust for auxiliary power unit and rear Sky Guardian housing; **6** FRL Mk 17B hose-and-drum unit in rear fuselage of K2/K3 only; **7** FRL Mk 32/2800 wing pod; **8** Rolls-Royce Conway turbofan (total four); **9** light grey camouflage replacing hemp (K2/K3) or white (C1) from 1994 onwards; **10** fuel receiver probe.

Notes: Recent conversion of 13 remaining C1s to C1(K) and five ex-BA Super VC10s to K4s, both versions having wing pods only. Total 14 C1s, five K2s, four K3s and five K4s purchased.

Below:

Westland Wessex HC2/HCC4

Support/SAR (HC2) and VVIP (HCC4) helicopter. Nos 22, 28, 32, 60, 72 and 84 Sqn, No 2 FTS and SARTS. **1** Port front position for optional Honeywell AN/AAR-47 missile approach warning receiver; **2** engine exhaust; **3** BAe infra-red jammer (optional); **4** position for starboard rear AN/AAR-47; **5** two-man hoist (300ft), starboard side of SAR aircraft; **6** two-seat cockpit with optional armour.

Notes: Options also include M130 flare dispensers and Nitesun searchlight. UK-based SAR HC2s are yellow; No 84 Sqn's HC2s are grey; Nos 60/72 Sqn adopted two-tone green in 1992; all-red HCC4s operated by No 32 (The Royal) Sqn. Total 72 HC2s and two HCC4s, of which 59/2 remain; five HC5Cs withdrawn 1994.

SECONDARY AIRCRAFT TYPES

Below:
BAe 780 Andover C1(PR)/E3
Calibration (illustrated); civilian contract operation. **1** Milligan Lamp for visibility on approach; **2** 'kneeling' main undercarriage for easier rear loading; **3** rear loading ramp; **4** red fin, central fuselage and engine nacelles; **5** Litton (Canada) Inc Inertially-Referenced Flight Inspection System for calibration; **6** Rolls-Royce Dart turboprop (total two); **7** two-man cockpit. *Notes:* Total 31 C1s built; four converted to E3 (and three to E3A, since withdrawn); two C1(PR) with under-fuselage camera bay (and sealed port freight door) for Open Skies Treaty overflights by monitoring unit based at Scampton.

Bottom:
BAe 125 Dominie T1/T2
Navigation trainer; No 6 FTS. **1** Ekco E190 radar, being replaced through T2 conversion programme by Thorn-EMI Super Searcher in nose stretched by 18 inches; **2** twin mainwheel undercarriage; **3** Rolls-Royce Viper 301 turbojet (total two); **4** two students and one instructor in cabin (revised design in T2); **5** dual control cockpit. *Notes:* All Dominies have a red and white colour scheme. Deliveries 20; 19 remain, of which 14 to be upgraded.

Top:
BAe 125 CC2/CC3
Communications; No 32 (The Royal) Sqn. **1** VIP interior; **2** Garrett TFE731 turbofan (total two); **3** Northrop MIRTS infra-red jammer (four aircraft only); **4** crew and passenger entrance (port side). *Notes:* All repainted from white to grey (illustrated); four CC1/BAe 125-400s withdrawn March 1994; CC2 is BAe 125-600; CC3 is BAe 125-700; CC1/CC2 retrofitted from Viper to CC3's Garrett engines. Total two CC2, six CC3 remain.

Above:
BAe 146 CC2
VVIP communications; No 32 Sqn. **1** Two-crew flight deck; **2** VVIP interior; **3** Lycoming ALF 504R-5 turbofan (total four); **4** 'petal' airbrakes form rear fuselage; **5** Northrop MIRTS infra-red jammers in pods; **6** rear passenger door. *Notes:* Total two C1s and three CC2s acquired; three CC2s remain.

Below:
British Aerospace Bulldog T1
Primary trainer; No 6 FTS, UASs (17), No 13 AEF, CFS. **1** Fixed undercarriage; **2** RAF College Cranwell blue band; **3** rearwards-sliding hood to dual control cockpit; **4** Textron Lycoming IO-360-A1B6 piston engine.
Notes: Total 130 bought; 115 remain.

Bottom:
De Havilland DHC-1 Chipmunk T10
Air experience/grading trainer; AEFs (12), CFS. **1** DH Gipsy Major 8 piston engine with cartridge starter; **2** fixed undercarriage; **3** tailwheel — unique in 'non-historic' RAF aircraft; **4** rear-sliding canopy; **5** optional glider-towing hook.
Notes: Total 740 acquired; 75 remain.

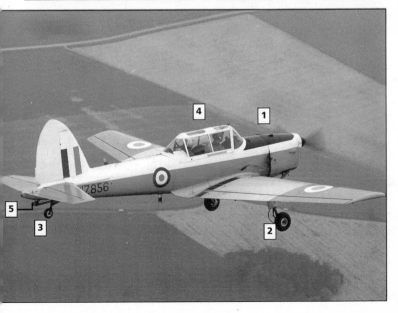

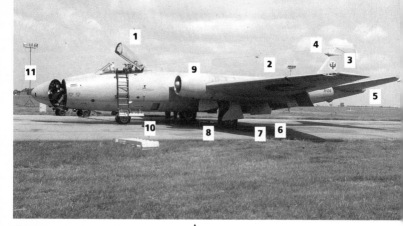

Above:

British Aircraft Corporation Canberra PR9

Photographic survey; No 39 (1 PRU) Sqn. **1** Single-seat cockpit offset to port; **2** wings of increased chord and span compared with earlier marks; **3** No 39 Sqn badge; **4** radar warning receiver forward antenna; **5** RWR rear antenna; **6** bay for vertical F96 camera (6in or 12in lens); **7** split pair of F96 cameras with 24in or 48in lenses; **8** Texas Instruments ARI 5936/3 infra-red linescan (optionally 'System 3' long-range oblique camera in bulged housing); **9** Rolls-Royce Avon Mk 206 turbojet (total two); **10** (port side only) oblique F96 camera (24 in or 28 in lens); **11** nose access to navigator's position.

Notes: Total 23 bought; five remain with No 39 Squadron (which also has two T4s and two PR7s).

Below:

Westland/Aerospatiale SA 341D Gazelle HT3

Training and communications helicopter; No 32 Sqn, No 2 FTS and CFS. **1** dual control with bench seat for three at rear; **2** Turbomeca Astazou III turboshaft engine; **3** transmission to tail rotor; **4** 'Fenestron' (or 'fan-in-fin') tail rotor; **5** fixed skid landing gear.

Notes: Total 30 built; 27 remain, plus four Navy HT2s on loan.

Top:
BAe 201 Jetstream T1
Twin-conversion and aircrew trainer; No 6 FTS. **1** Dual control cockpit; **2** cabin with four passenger seats; **3** Turbomeca Astazou XVID turboprop (total two); **4** markings of No 45 (Reserve) Sqn.
Notes: 26 acquired; 11 remain.

Above:
Shorts S312 Tucano T1
Basic trainer; Nos 1, 3 and 6 FTSs, and CFS. **1** Garrett TPE331-12B turboshaft engine; **2** two-piece canopy covering student and (in raised rear cockpit) instructor; **3** airbrake (in retracted position); **4** twin exhausts add 51hp in equivalent thrust; **5** RAF Cranwell blue band.
Notes: Aircraft serving No 6 FTS have staff pilot in front cockpit and student navigator in rear. Total 130 procured; one lost.

Top:
Grob 109B Vigilant T1
Power-assisted (self-launching) sailplane; Nos 612, 613, 616, 624, 632, 633, 635, 637, 642, 644 and 663 VGSs, ACCGS and CFS. **1** Two-seat, side-by-side cockpit; **2** glass fibre construction; **3** fixed and spatted undercarriage; **4** downwards view window; **5** 75hp Limbach piston engine; **6** non-standard presentation of serial.
Notes: 53 bought; all remain.

Above:
Grob 103 Viking T1
Sailplane; Nos 611, 614, 615, 617, 618, 621, 622, 625, 626, 627, 631, 634, 636, 645, 661 and 662 VGSs, ACCGS and CFS. **1** Auxiliary nosewheel; **2** mainwheel; **3** auxiliary tailwheel; **4** skids on wingtips; **5** T-tail; **6** two-seat, tandem cockpit; **7** attachment for towing cable.
Notes: Winch-launched. Total 100 bought; 95 remain.

OTHER AIRCRAFT

Below:
Pilatus/Britten-Norman Islander CC2/CC2A
One of each variant with Northolt Station Flight.

Bottom:
De Havilland Devon C2/2
One aircraft with Battle of Britain Memorial Flight.

Below:
Schleicher ASW-19 Valiant T1
Four aircraft with ACCGS.

Bottom:
Schempp-Hirth Janus C
Two aircraft with ACCGS.

Note:
Not included in this résumé are several ex-RAF aircraft used by research establishments and civil-registered aircraft under RAF contract.

HISTORIC AIRCRAFT

Top:
Hawker Hurricane IIC
Battle of Britain Memorial Flight.

Above:
Supermarine 390 Spitfire PRXIX
Battle of Britain Memorial Flight.

Above:
Avro 683 Lancaster BI
Battle of Britain Memorial Flight.

Below:
Douglas C-47 Dakota C4
Battle of Britain Memorial Flight.

THINGS TO COME
Aircraft scheduled to enter service in the years ahead.

Top:
Lockheed C-130J Hercules II
Commitment in December 1994 to order 25 aircraft, with deliveries to begin to A&AEE in September 1996 and to Lyneham six months later. Will replace half current Hercules C1/C3 fleet; Airbus FLA is a contender for second-batch purchase early in next century. *Lockheed*

Above:
European Helicopter Industries EH 101
An official announcement on 9 March 1995 confirmed that the RAF is to obtain 22 EH 101s (possibly designated Griffin HC1) built at Yeovil by Westland from 1999

Below:
Eurofighter 2000
UK commitment to 250 to replace Tornado F3 in air defence and Jaguar fighter-bombers. Production deliveries from 2000; first squadron to form in 2002-2003.

AIR LAUNCHED MISSILES AND GUIDED BOMBS

Below:
British Aerospace ALARM
'Air-Launched Anti-Radar Missile.' Carried by Tornado GR1.

Opposite above:
British Aerospace Sea Eagle
Sea-skimming anti-ship missile. Carried by Tornado GR1B.

Opposite centre:
British Aerospace Sky Flash
Semi-active radar homing AAM. Carried by Tornado F3. (Similar-shaped Raytheon AIM-7E2 Sparrow held in reserve.) *British Aerospace*

Opposite bottom:
McDonnell Douglas AGM-84A Harpoon
Anti-ship missile carried internally by Nimrod MR2.

Below:
Bodenseewerk Gerätetechnik AIM-9L Sidewinder
Infra-red-homing AAM. Carried offensively by Tornado F3 and Hawk T1A; for self-defence by Harrier and Jaguar; and applicable to Nimrod MR2. BAe ASRAAM ordered as replacement.

Bottom:
Paveway II
Laser-guided bomb. RAF 1,000lb bomb, Mks 13-22, fitted with CPU-123/B nose guidance unit and Mk 120 pop-out rear fins. Paveway III ordered in 1994 as replacement.

4 Aircraft identity markings

Identification is of great importance in the military world. Aircraft of the RAF are always marked with the internationally recognised national colours of the United Kingdom and a serial number; optionally they may wear the badge of their operating unit, an individual letter or number assigned by that operator and other special markings.

NATIONAL MARKINGS

International convention requires military aircraft to signify their country of origin in a recognised manner. The UK applies a circular device which, on non-combatant aircraft, includes the national colours of red (in the centre), white and blue. This is generally described as a roundel, although 'cockade' (normally associated with the French, in whose markings the order of the colours is reversed) is more correct. In heraldry, a roundel is a disc of one colour, so the UK's marking is actually three roundels of different size, superimposed.

The usual style of non-tactical roundel presentation is currently Type D, in which the colours are symmetrical: if 'd' is the diameter of the whole (ie, blue), then white is two-thirds 'd' and red is one-third 'd'. Tactical aircraft omit the white because this high-visibility colour would compromise their camouflage. Such roundels are termed Type B but, again, that is not wholly correct. The original Type B of World War 2 had the red centre of two-fifths of diameter, whereas in the modern version it is one-half.

Aircraft of the RAF (but not the Fleet Air Arm or Army Air Corps) have a fin flash of red/white/blue or red/blue to correspond with the roundel. The proportions of fin flashes vary considerably: an upright rectangle, a square, a horizontal rectangle or any of the aforementioned in 'swept-back' style. The degree of 'sweep-back' often conforms to the angle of fin or rudder leading edge and therefore varies from aircraft to aircraft. It should be noted that fin flashes are 'handed' so that the red is nearest the nose on both sides. Aircraft wearing light coloured camouflage will have pale red and blue in their roundels and flashes.

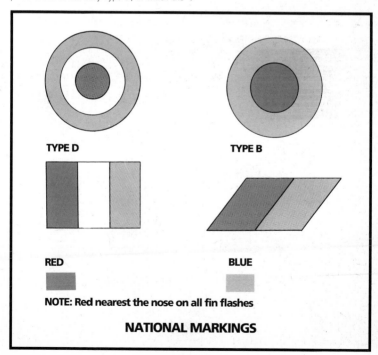

TYPE D

TYPE B

RED

BLUE

NOTE: Red nearest the nose on all fin flashes

NATIONAL MARKINGS

MILITARY SERIALS

Recently there has been a fundamental change in the unified system of serials for UK military aircraft. The present two-letters-plus-three-digits form was introduced in 1940, and most serving RAF aircraft are now in the batches XA100-XZ999 and ZA101-ZZ999 (omitting letters C, I, O, Q, U, and Y). In 1937, the 'broken blocks' system of leaving gaps ('blackouts') in, and between batches of serials was adopted to confuse foreign intelligence agencies.

Now that most aircraft orders are officially revealed, broken blocks serve no useful purpose — especially when they are assigned to aircraft built for export, which are required to have UK military serials for flight-test. In recent years, these export serials have outnumbered aircraft bought for the UK armed forces, although a relaxation of rules has resulted in target drones no longer being given regular serials.

The consequences of the momentous decision late in 1993 — to abandon broken blocks and allocate UK military serials in unbroken sequence — are only now becoming apparent. Numbers assigned since then have been as below:

- ZH758-ZH761 final 'blackout'
- ZH762   Skyship 600   Army
- ZH763   OneEleven 539m   DSRA
- ZH764-ZH774 not known
- ZH775-ZH777 Chinook HC2   RAF
- ZH778-ZH795 Hawk Mk 208   Malaysia
- ZH796-ZH813 Sea Harrier FRS2   Navy
- ZH814-ZH816 Bell 212   Army
- ZH817-ZH820 Hawk Mk 63   Abu Dhabi

A complete listing of current UK military aircraft and an explanation of their serial number systems appears in abc *Military Aircraft Markings* published annually by Ian Allan Ltd.

Opposite above:
Illustrative of several themes, this Tornado F3 tail bears a standard military serial number; a Type B ('raked-back' version) fin flash in low-visibility pale red and blue; a squadron badge (No 43); and code letters indicating squadron (G) and individual aircraft (C). *Paul Jackson*

Opposite below:
Hunter T7 XL577 also wears its 'maintenance serial' 8676M and is part of the small fleet of theoretically airworthy Hunters maintained by the Servicing Instruction Flight at Cranwell. The SIF badge is an owl wearing a mortar board, flanked by red and white bars, and it has the alternative and entirely fictional title of 'No 284 (Training) Sqn'. *Paul Jackson*

Aircraft grounded for instructional purposes are normally assigned a new serial (though many do not wear it) suffixed 'M'. This series, which has no blackouts, is approaching 9300M. Almost 300 aircraft have current M-serials for a variety of tasks at various MoD installations throughout the country, whilst some 200 more are on static display as 'gate guardians' and museum exhibits. Included in the latter are aircraft of foreign origin which have been given 'shadow' identities, one of the most bizarre being 8583M for a V-1 flying bomb.

CODES

Within an individual unit, an aircraft's full serial number is generally only of interest to those responsible for compiling maintenance records. For most other purposes, a single letter or number will suffice as an 'in-house' identity. As most combat squadrons have 12 aircraft, the letters of the alphabet are adequate and generally used. Training units with over 26 machines often adopt fleet numbers or sometimes the 'last-three' of the serial.

Whilst the above-mentioned systems usually begin at 'A' and '1' (or '01'), there are exceptions. If two squadrons are sharing the same station, they may take different halves of the alphabet. Extending this further, almost the entire fleets of certain tactical aircraft have two-letter codes, the first of which identifies the operator. Because of equipment exchanges between squadrons, such two-letter codes are not permanently wedded to a serial number. Tornado GR1 codes were allocated in batches to RAF Germany operating bases in squadron number order, whereas Tornado F3 codes were assigned alphabetically in chronological order of squadron conversion to the type.

Tornado GR1

● AA-AZ	No IX Sqn, Brüggen
● BA-BZ	No 14 Sqn, Brüggen
● CA-CZ	No 17 Sqn, Brüggen
● DA-DZ	No 31 Sqn, Brüggen
● EA-EZ	No XV Sqn, Laarbruch*
● FA-FZ	No 16 Sqn, Laarbruch*
● FA-FZ	No 12 Sqn, Lossiemouth
● GA-GZ	No 20 Squadron, Laarbruch*
● HA-HZ	reserved (for No 2 Sqn? — uses A-Z)
● JA-JZ	No 27 Sqn, Marham*
● KA-KZ	reserved (for No 13 Sqn? — uses A-Z)
● LA-LZ	reserved (for No 45 Sqn?*)
● MA-MZ	No 617 Sqn, Marham*
● TA-TZ	No XV (R) Sqn, Lossiemouth

*Disbanded or relocated
No 617 now uses the World War 2 codes AJ-A to AJ-Z, whilst No 12 reuses the FA-FZ series to reflect its badge: F for fox.

65

Tornado F3

● AA-AZ	OCU, Coningsby
● A1-A9	OCU 'overflow' 1991-
● BA-BZ	No 29 Sqn, Coningsby
● CA-CZ	No 5 Sqn, Coningsby
● DA-DZ	No 11 Sqn, Leeming
● EA-EZ	No 23 Sqn, Leeming*
● FA-FZ	No 25 Sqn, Leeming
● GA-GZ	No 43 Sqn, Leuchars
● HA-HZ	No 111 Sqn, Leuchars

*Disbanded

Jaguar GR1A

● EA-EZ	No 6 Sqn, Coltishall
● FA-FZ	No 41 Sqn, Coltishall
● GA-GZ	No 54 Sqn, Coltishall
	(AA-DZ previously used by
	Nos 14, 17, 20 and 31 Sqn
	before receiving Tornados)

Harrier GR7

● AA-AZ	No 3 Sqn, Gütersloh
● CA-CZ	No IV Sqn, Gütersloh
● WA-WX	Operation 'Warden'
	detachment, Incirlik (Turkey)

Hawk

● CA-CZ	No 100 Sqn
● DA-DZ	No 234 (R), later 208 (R)
	Sqn/4 FTS
● PA-PZ	CFS Squadron, later No 19
	(R)/4 FTS
● TA-TZ	No 74 (R) Sqn/4 FTS

The No 4 FTS elements based their code ranges on the badges or crests of the original components: D for dragon (234), P for pelican (CFS) and T for tiger (No 74).

Support helicopters

● BA-BZ	No 18 Sqn (Chinook/Puma)
● CA-CZ	No 33 Sqn (Puma)
● DA-DZ	No 230 Sqn (Puma)
● EA-EZ	No 7 Sqn (Chinook)
● FA-FZ	No 27 (R) Sqn (both)

Canberra

● AA-AZ	No 39 (1 PRU) Sqn
● BA-BZ	No 231 OCU
● CA-CZ	No 100 Sqn
● EA-EZ	No 360 Sqn

(No 39 retains its codes despite being the only remaining Canberra unit; No 100 still uses CA-CZ on its Hawks.)

Squadrons assigned a trainer version of their front-line type will usually apply the code 'T' or '-T'. Additional trainers may use 'X-Z'. More inventive units select letters to allow their aircraft to spell names — for example 'SHINY TWO II AC' (AC — Army Co-operation) for No II Sqn and 'TIGER SQN' for No 74. A few University Air Squadrons have caught the bug, such as C-U-A-S and L-U-A-S at Cambridge and Liverpool, as has No 8 Air Experience Flight: 8-A-E-F. More subtle

still are the different coloured propeller spinners used by Glasgow & Strathclyde UAS and Queen's UAS; and No 84 Sqn's unique system of identifying its five Wessex by playing card symbols: heart, club, spade, diamond and joker.

A practice which is now a shadow of its former self is the application of 'personal codes' to aircraft by squadron commanders and more senior officers. Examples during the past decade have included Lightning F6 XR728 'JS' (Gp Capt John Spencer, Binbrook CO); and Phantom FGR2s of No 56 Sqn, XV420 'BT' (Wg Cdr Barry Titchen) and XV470 'BD' (Wg Cdr Barry Doggett). Those for whom their squadron's legitimate double-letter codes have been fortuitously assigned have included Wg Cdr Alfie Ferguson of No IX Sqn (Tornado GR1 ZD892 'AF') and Wg Cdr David Hamilton of No XI Sqn (Tornado F3 ZE764 'DH'). Another F3, ZE858 was marked 'FK' by the Leeming Aircraft Servicing Flight when it arrived in advance of No 25 Sqn's formation; and ground training Canberra TT18 WK127 was painted 'F-O' at Wyton. The origin of these last two codes is better imagined than described. The sole current example of a genuine personal code is Tornado F3 ZE889 'SB' of the ADOEU (F3OEU), flown by Wg Cdr Stuart Black.

BADGES

Badges assigned to RAF units are frequently and incorrectly described as 'crests' or even 'coats of arms'. The only proper name is badge, and many badges have an interesting origin which repays study. Badges must be approved by the College of Arms — the current Inspector of RAF Badges

Opposite top:
Liver Bird. The famous symbol of Liverpool is to be found on the Bulldogs of LUAS. Bars are medium blue, white and black. *Paul Jackson*

Opposite middle:
A wing commander's pennant is but one of many markings applied to the forward fuselage of this Harrier. Also to be seen are No 1 Sqn's winged '1' badge and (as is common practice on aircraft types also operated by No 2 Group) safety instructions in German as well as English. Vertical black lines are toe-guides to 'kick-in' steps and the six light rectangles are low-intensity lights for night formation-keeping. *Paul Jackson*

Opposite below:
Not all badges are officially recognised by the College of Arms. Cambridge-based Chipmunks of No 5 AEF have a winged Roman 'V' beneath an Astral Crown. *Paul Jackson*

HERE

WG CDR I R HARVEY

NORMAL CANOPY OPEN ENTRIEGELUNG

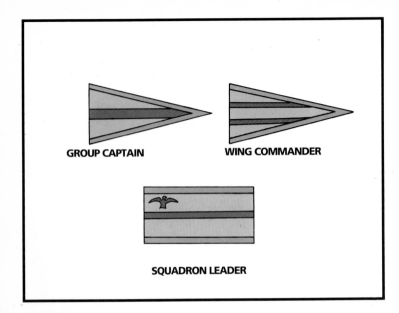

GROUP CAPTAIN

WING COMMANDER

SQUADRON LEADER

being the Surrey Herald of Arms — and comprise a subject surrounded by a wreath of leaves, surmounted by a crown and with a motto in a scroll beneath. The original grant is signed by the monarch of the day and the Inspector, the first such approvals taking place in May 1936.

Rarely is the full badge applied to an aircraft, normal procedure being to display the subject — such as the Greek 'π' and Maltese cross of No 22 Sqn. (Malta because the squadron was based there when it applied for a badge; 'π' because as part of No 7 Wing in World War 1 it had '22/7' on a board above its HQ's entrance — and 22/7 equals 'π' in circular arithmetic.) A very few units use an unauthorised device to proclaim their identity: No 6 Sqn's badge is an eagle preying on a serpent, but its aircraft are marked with a winged can-opener to recall its tank-busting success in World War 2 as well as a Royal Artillery 'gunner's stripe' on the fin from its days in army co-operation.

In the case of a subject which has a recognisable front and back (ie, it faces in one direction — invariably to the left on the badge), that representation will be applied to the port (left) side of the aircraft. A mirror image is painted on the starboard, so that — for example — in the case of No 11 Squadron's two eagles, they are not seen to be flying backwards at Mach 2 on the right side of Tornado F3s.

The only RAF flying unit to have a grant of arms (rather than a badge) and apply it in full to its aircraft is the Central Flying School. It is therefore correct to refer to CFS aircraft carrying the unit's arms (or coat of arms). However, the reference under Hawk codes (above) to the CFS crest *is not* in error as the pelican is but one (the topmost) part of the unit's full grant of arms (crest, crown, helmet, shield, mantle and motto). UAS Bulldogs are often marked with part of their University's arms, but in the form of an approved badge. Outside the RAF, the A&AEE has arms — of which part are displayed in the form of an unapproved badge — as does the ETPS.

OTHER MARKINGS

Camouflage is the most obvious additional marking to be found on tactical aircraft. Low-level operators use dark green and dark sea grey, and if the undersides of their aircraft are similarly painted, they are said to have 'wrap-around' camouflage. Addition to this of black serials and titles, plus Type B roundels produces a 'low-viz' (visibility) colour scheme. Air defence fighters use medium-level camouflage of three light greys: medium sea grey, mixed grey (known as Barley grey after its deviser, Phil Barley) and light grey. Large aircraft (VC10 K2/K3, Nimrod and Victor) wear a colour known as hemp which is to afford obscurity when parked on toned-down concrete. In 1994, the first VC10 appeared in the grey colour scheme, implying that the main threat to the aircraft's security is now perceived to be in the air and not an attack upon its base.

During the late 1980s and early 1990s, medium grey became popular with BAe 125s, Wessex, Jaguars, Hercules, Harriers and Buccaneers. After the last-mentioned were withdrawn, replacement Tornado GR1Bs began adopting a darker shade of grey to match the sea. Only in the case of the 125 was the entire fleet repainted. For the Gulf War, a sandy-pink washable paint was applied to several types of aircraft and it invariably became known as 'Pink Panther' or 'Desert Pink'. In correct nomenclature 'washable' is ARTF — Alkali-Removable Temporary Finishing.

Training aircraft are painted red and white for high conspicuity, but a recent and curious development has been the adoption of overall gloss black for Hawks. In a series of trials during 1992 it was established that black provides the best colour contrast with the average cloud, and so repainting began in earnest during 1994.

Insignia of rank will be seen on the cockpit sides of some aircraft. Since the 1960s, officers' ranks have been out of step with their responsibilities due to a general upgrading. Group Captains captain wings; Wing Commanders command squadrons; and Squadron Leaders lead

Below opposite:
The Central Flying School is the only RAF flying unit to have a grant of arms. *Paul Jackson*

Right:
Station badges are rarely to be found on aircraft, but Northolt's adorns the Gazelles of No 32 Sqn. *Paul Jackson*

flights. A 12-aircraft squadron is usually divided into 'A' and 'B' Flights, each run by an officer of Squadron Leader rank, who will paint a rectangular flag ('air force blue' with red and royal blue horizontal stripes) on his aircraft. The squadron's commander will apply a Wing Commander's triangular pennant, containing two thin red stripes — or, in the rare, but unknown, case of a squadron being led by a Group Captain, a pennant with one broad red stripe.

Finally — and hardly liable to be missed — are the special colour schemes applied for anniversaries, and on aircraft chosen for solo aerobatic displays from season to season. Fortunately for the enthusiast (and the shareholders of Agfa, Fuji and Kodak) most units need little prompting to produce a specially-marked aircraft which can be seen around the air show circuit.

RADIO IDENTITIES

Call-signs used by military aircraft rarely are related to their serial number and will usually change after every flight. Several systems are in use by the RAF, of which the most common is the tri-graph of three letters or a number and two letters (followed by two numbers to indicate the individual aircraft). A typical example is 'Q9Y 15' for a Tornado F3 of No 111 Sqn. Whilst this system can, and does, use any combination at random, training units tend to use a permanent tri-graph closely related to the name of their base. Examples are:

● COT	TTTE, Cottesmore
● CWL	No 3 FTS, Cranwell
● FYT	No 6 FTS, Finningley
● FYY	No 6 FTS, Finningley
● LON	No 1 FTS, Linton-on-Ouse
● LOP	No 1 FTS, Linton-on-Ouse
● LOS	Nos 15/16 (R) Sqn, Lossiemouth
● ODM	No 27 (R) Sqn, Odiham
● SAP	CFS, Scampton
● SYS	No 2 FTS, Shawbury
● VYT	No 4 FTS, Valley

In similar vein, University Air Squadrons use the series UAA, UAB, *et seq* and Air Experience Flights are AEA, AEB, etc.

Transports often use a four-figure number prefixed 'RRR' or 'Ascot' and tactical squadrons on non-operational flights can use a name, instead of a trigraph. Such names are sometimes related to the unit's badge, and are marked with an asterisk in the list of examples below:

● 'Arcade'	No II Sqn
● 'Balsa'	No 6 FTS Hawk Sqn
● 'Civic'	SAOEU
● 'Phoenix'*	No 56 (R) Sqn
● 'Fresco'	No 23 Sqn
● 'Snake'	No 14 Sqn
● 'Taragon'	No 43 Sqn
● 'Tiger'*	No 74 (R) Sqn
● 'Wildcat'*	No 20 (R) Sqn

Some words have become well known as call-signs, perhaps the most widely-recognised being those for The Queen's Flight: 'Kittyhawk' for VVIPs; 'Kitty' for VIPs and 'Rainbow' for other flights. Further samples, at random, include:

● 'Blackbox'	DRA
● 'Gauntlet'	Boscombe Down (A&AEE, ETPS, SAOEU)
● 'Nugget'	DRA
● 'Magic'	all E-3 Sentries
● 'Metman'	Met Research Flight (also 'Snoopy')
● 'Teebird'	DERA Llanbedr
● 'Tester'	ETPS

The list is endless… but that is the reason for call-signs.

Below:
Tornado F3

5 The RAF in action

Having trained for four decades to play its part in an all-out nuclear war against the Warsaw Pact, the RAF has spent the last five years performing a different, but related role. Skills perfected in anticipation of defending the UK from Russian long-range bombers or penetrating the formidable defences of the Iron Curtain have recently been exercised in other skies. The collapse of Communism in Europe has lifted the threat of nuclear annihilation, but the armed forces of NATO have had little time to rest since the Warsaw Pact was dissolved. Hopes of a new World order were dashed almost as soon as they had been voiced in the heady excitement of the Berlin Wall's demolition.

With Superpower confrontation at an end, smaller players were emboldened to make their bids for power. First came Iraq's invasion of Kuwait in August 1990. RAF aircraft were amongst the first to reinforce Saudi Arabia against a follow-on attack and participated conspicuously in the war of January-February 1991 which evicted Iraqi forces from their briefly-held prize. The decision not to subjugate Iraq completely has left unfinished business and a requirement to base combat aircraft close to both the northern and southern areas of the country to prevent Saddam Hussein slaughtering more of his own citizens.

Nearer to home, compassion for the plight of the people of former Yugoslavia prompted another large-scale international operation in which the UK played its part through NATO. Acting as a police force attempting to guarantee relief supplies and protect civilians in Bosnia, NATO was subject to daily control from UN diplomats, and its inability to pursue clear-cut military objectives without hindrance was a cause of great frustration. More satisfaction could be taken from the airlift of vital food and medicine to Bosnia by Hercules operating daily schedules in the face of possible attack by SAMs and small-arms. Equally appreciated was the food airlift in Somalia which averted further famine when all authority collapsed in 1992, and the ferrying of ground forces to support the UN in Rwanda during 1994.

Major operations involving the RAF since 1990 are given below. The long-term overseas policing missions receive no compensatory funding and cut deeply into training schedules. Air- and ground-crews are normally provided by squadrons in rotation.

Operation 'Cheshire'
Relief flights to Sarajevo; Hercules C1 at Zagreb from 3 July 1992; transferred to Ancona from 14 February 1993; continuing in 1995.

Operation 'Gabriel'
Airlift of troops and equipment by Hercules to Rwanda for relief operations, beginning 1 August 1994.

Operation 'Granby'
The Gulf War and its associated build-up and withdrawal phases, August 1990 to July 1991.

Operation 'Grapple'
Policing 'no-fly' zone of Bosnia (NATO Operation Deny Flight) and protecting UN troops (NATO Operation Disciplined Guard); Tornado F3 from 18 April 1993, plus Jaguar GR1A from 16 July.

Below:
The Jaguar force has been deeply involved with the Gulf War, Operation 'Warden' over northern Iraq and Operation 'Grapple' over Bosnia and has only been off duty for three months between August 1990 and 1995. Duties for 'Warden' and 'Grapple' have centred on reconnaissance with (illustrated) centreline pods. *Paul Jackson*

1993, both at Gioia del Colle, Italy; VC10 tankers at Malpensa; TriStar from June 1993, but to Pisa in October 1993; attack missions flown November 1994; patrols continuing in 1995.

Operation 'Hampden'
Reconnaissance of Bosnia by Canberra PR9s operating from Wyton and Marham. No details released; 1993 onwards.

Operation 'Jural'
Policing of southern Iraq, south of 32°N (US Operation Southern Watch). Tornado GR1/GR1A at Dhahran, Saudi Arabia, from 27 August 1992; tanker support (VC10 assisted by Victor until September 1993 at Bahrain). Attack missions flown January 1993; patrols continuing in 1995.

Operation 'Vigour'
Famine relief in Somalia (US Operation Restore Hope); Hercules C1 at Mombasa, Kenya; December 1992 to April 1993.

Operation 'Warden'
Policing of northern Iraq (north of 36°N) from Incirlik, Turkey (US Operation Provide Comfort). Jaguar GR1A from 4 September 1991; replaced by Harrier GR7 from 1 April 1993; tanker support (Victor, then VC10 from January 1992) from Akrotiri, Cyprus, then Incirlik from February 1992; continuing in 1995.

In addition, RAF Nimrod MR2s have been involved in enforcing the arms embargo on former Yugoslavia in the international Operation Maritime Guard (initially Maritime Monitor, between July and November 1992; WEU name Sharp Fence); and Sentry AEW1s have undertaken patrols for Deny Flight (Sky Monitor before 12 April 1993) as well as supporting Maritime Monitor/Guard.

QUICK REACTION ALERT (INTERCEPTOR)

'Q', as it is usually known, has diminished in importance since the ending of the Cold War, but still represents the first line of air defence for the UK. Although foreign aircraft may fly within three miles of the coast without infringing British sovereignty, they will long before have appeared on NATO radar screens. Civil and military aircraft which have filed a flight plan may proceed at will; those which have not may find themselves with a free escort service provided by the RAF.

Whilst NATO is a skeletal organisation in peacetime (that is to say, its earmarked forces are under national control until the transition to war), there is one exception in the form of the air defence force. Here, all members exchange information, so that, for example, if a long-range maritime reconnaissance aircraft takes off from northern Russia and passes westwards through Norwegian airspace, the RAF will be aware of its movements well before it arrives at the borders of the UK Air Defence Region (UKADR) or comes

within range of the radar site on the Faroe Islands (see Chapter 7).

There were previously two principal categories of Russian tourist: maritime reconnaissance aircraft (usually the Tupolev Tu-142 *Bear*) flying north of Scotland to reach the Atlantic, and electronic intelligence aircraft (often Tupolev Tu-16 *Badgers*) investigating the East Coast radar defences. Having reached a peak in the early-1980s, numbers of both types of airspace penetration fell thereafter and the last interception by RAF fighters was undertaken on 6 September 1991. The next known reconnaissance flghts in northern waters did not take place until 9 and 17 September 1993 (at the time of a NATO exercise), although the aircraft turned back before entering the RAF area of responsibility.

As a consequence, the QRA(I) effort has been scaled down since 1990. Where once a northern and a southern RAF fighter station maintained 'Q', only Leuchars now does so, this arrangement coming into force on 9 January 1992. Crews from the other squadrons provide assistance on a rotation basis. The alert posture is matched by a VC10 at Brize Norton which can also be scrambled to provide support.

At the time of writing, the RAF's Tornado F3 force was practising its skills over Bosnia, enforcing the 'no-fly' zone. Here, the procedure

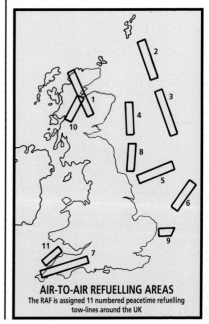

AIR-TO-AIR REFUELLING AREAS
The RAF is assigned 11 numbered peacetime refuelling tow-lines around the UK

was different, in that fighter aircraft of several nations were dispatched on a rota basis to undertake standing patrols under the direction of a USAF, NATO, RAF or French E-3 Sentry AWACS. Needless to relate, the vast majority of these missions were uneventful and the few alerts resulted in a frustrating search for armed trainers or helicopters taking full advantage of mountainous terrain and low flying for concealment.

AIR-TO-AIR REFUELING

Now an essential aspect of daily operations, AAR began in the RAF as a means of deploying bombers world-wide in the 1950s and rapidly spread to tactical forces, including air defence. Converted bombers — Valiants, Victors and a few Vulcans — were the first principal tanker aircraft, but that era ended with retirement of the last Victor squadron in October 1993. The regular tanker force now comprises five VC10 K2s, four VC10 K3s and five VC10 K4s which will be augmented, when required, by two TriStar K1s, four TriStar KC1 tanker/transports and 13 VC10 C1(K)s. It is planned to place three VC10s in storage as surplus to requirements. Additionally, six Hercules were converted to C1(K) tankers for support of air defence fighters in the Falkland Islands, one later reverting to a transport.

The VC10 C1(K)s are best described as 'transports with tanker capability' because, unlike the TriStar, they have insufficient tankage to refuel a pair of fighters *and* carry their support crews and equipment over a long distance. If Argentina again threatened to invade the Falkland Islands, TriStars could bring both two reinforcement aircraft and 250 or so personnel on the same flight.

Above:
The Russian submarines may have gone home, but the RAF's Nimrod MR2s continue to patrol the UK's waters in addition to assisting in enforcement of the Maritime Guard arms embargo off former Yugoslavia. *Paul Jackson*

Here is the distinction between tanker and tanker/transport operations. Day-to-day, tankers are positioned on racetrack-shaped 'tow-lines' over the sea and sparsely-populated areas of land. Interceptor, attack, maritime reconnaissance, AEW and even transport aircraft can book a time-slot to practise refuelling which may, at some future date, become an operational necessity. Additionally, of course, one AAR can almost double the endurance of an aircraft. In one sortie, therefore, a tactical aircraft can accomplish more training without the unnecessary and wasteful transit flight between base and the exercise area. Tankers will routinely be dispatched on a 'trail' to take aircraft abroad, such as to the USA for 'Red Flag' or Canada for 'Maple Flag' exercises; to Cyprus or Decimomannu for weapons and combat training; or further afield on less frequent deployments. In the Gulf War, Victors, VC10s and TriStar K1s were used to support combat missions by Tornados and Jaguars and the two last-mentioned continued to do so for Operation 'Deny Flight'/'Grapple' over Bosnia.

Finally, there is 'do-it-yourself' tanking in the form of the 'buddy-buddy' system in which a small refuelling pod is attached to a strike/attack aircraft. The RAF acquired 15 Sargeant-Fletcher 28-300 pods for Tornados during the Gulf War, but had no cause to use them. Instead, FRL Mk 20 pods from retired Victors are expected to be fitted instead to Tornado GR1Bs operating in the anti-shipping role out of Lossiemouth.

HARDENED AIRCRAFT SHELTER OPERATIONS

The HAS first was used by NATO in Europe during the mid-1970s and came to RAF bases in the UK when Honington's first site was opened in November 1981 (for No IX Sqn and its Tornados). The typical site comprises 12 Phase 3 shelters, a Personnel Briefing Facility (PBF) and a Hardened Personnel Shelter (HPS). Two separate sites per station is the norm.

The arched HAS is made of reinforced concrete and can protect two Tornado-sized aircraft (three at a squeeze) from a near miss by a 1,000lb bomb. Two flat steel doors are slid back to allow aircraft to leave their HAS and two smaller doors at the rear are opened to allow hot gases to escape through a bifurcated 'chimney' when the aircraft starts its engines. Attached to the side of the building is a similarly reinforced Aerospace Ground Annexe (AGE) with storage space and room for a fuel tanker to drive in. (In RAF Germany, there are many Phase 1 HASs still in use, modified with an AGE, but identifiable by their smaller size — one Tornado or two Jaguars — and the hinged, shell-shaped doors which open beneath a roof overhang, or 'porch'.) The UK's last HAS site was also at Honington, handed over to No 13 Sqn in January 1990 and also of note in being the sole installation with the slightly larger Phase 4 HAS.

The PBF functions as a squadron HQ. It comprises a main, reinforced and windowless area, plus a 'soft' section, which would be abandoned in wartime, with offices and a rest-room/coffee bar. Air-locks, a decontamination area and air filtering system make the PBF proof against chemical warfare and radioactive dust.

Bottom:
The final HAS site built in the UK was of Phase 4 shelters on the northwestern corner of Honington. Note the deliberately random positioning of buildings to complicate air attack. *RAF*

Above:
The same installation pictured from directly above by a Tornado GR1A's infra-red linescan camera. This gives horizon-to-horizon cover (left and right of the print) but distorts straight lines into curves. The hard-copy picture is a printout from video tape, but even the original does not give as much detail as a photograph. However, linescan is unaffected by night, so the Tornado can operate at low level under cover of darkness. *RAF*

Naturally, such precautions are not taken routinely, but the regular exercises to which all units are submitted ensure that personnel are practised in NBC (Nuclear, Biological and Chemical) precautions. For aircrew, this means protective body clothing and the Cam Lock AR5 respirator system which covers the entire head before venturing outside. Until plugged into the aircraft's oxygen, aircrew carry a hand-held, battery-powered air filter nicknamed the 'whistling handbag.'

Ground personnel are issued with the same basic type of NBC-protective clothing (the Mk 4 'Noddy Suit') and a respirator — originally the S6, but increasingly the new S10. Contrary to popular belief, the HAS is not NBC-proof for the good reason that it has to open its doors for an aircraft to leave. Furthermore, even if the air base had not been under attack, aircraft could return having flown through a cloud of contamination. Off-duty personnel of all ranks would be accommodated in the HPS during war, but this dormitory and feeding area is the one facility which is not used on a day-to-day basis.

The HAS and PBF are thereby placing a strain on maintenance facilities, compared with the traditional system of servicing aircraft in one large hangar (which is, of course, an ideal target for one large bomb). More personnel and tools are needed in the HAS regime, and now that the risk of air attack on the UK is diminished, it may be that some scaling-down of hardened operations could be authorised.

ARMAMENT AND AIR COMBAT PRACTICE

As the age of air-to-air missiles dawned, it was predicted that the cannon would rapidly disappear from interceptor aircraft. Indeed, the later marks of Lightning dispensed with what was regarded as an anachronism — only to have two ADENs fitted to the front of the F6's fuel tanks in middle age. No such mistake has been made with the Tornado F3, which has a 27mm IWKA-Mauser on the starboard side (the GR1 has two) and an advanced air data and sighting computer which makes it highly accurate in close combat.

NATO requires each interceptor pilot to prove his marksmanship annually by putting a specified number of holes through a banner target under controlled conditions of distance and flight pattern. This must be done twice within six consecutive sorties to gain an ACE qualification — not 'ace' as in shooting down five enemy aircraft, but ACE as in Allied Command Europe. The banner is 6ft high and 30ft long, but appears as only 12ft in length because of the acute angle of approach.

The uncertain British weather could disrupt qualification shoots, so each squadron in turn deploys with tanker support to Akrotiri for a three-week APC (Armament Practice Camp). Target towing is by No 100 Sqn, which has a permanent detachment of Hawks in Cyprus during the shooting season.

Another yearly excursion is to Valley, in Anglesey. At the Strike Command Air-to-Air Missile Establishment, live weapons are fired at targets towed behind GAF Jindivik Mk 104B drones launched from Llanbedr and monitored by Range Control at Aberporth. Sometimes a Northrop Chukar D2 is used and very occasionally a Beech Stiletto released from under the wing of a specially equipped Canberra. Because of the high cost of even the Sidewinder AAM, squadrons are only allowed up to six missile launches per year, each round carrying a telemetry transmitter to allow later analysis of its performance.

In addition to set camps, squadrons may be called to fire missiles in short notice exercises at Valley. Most heart-stopping of all, QRA fighters will occasionally be launched as if 'for real' and find themselves directed to Cardigan Bay for an appointment with a Jindivik. In this and the short-notice exercise, live missiles from the squadron's stock are used. Aircraft which use the Sidewinder for self defence are also visitors to STCAAME: Harrier, Jaguar and Tornado GR1.

For practice in the skills of air fighting, squadrons deploy to a third location. The NATO Air Combat Manoeuvring Installation at Decimomannu, Sardinia (for short, 'Decci' — pronounced deh-chee) is used by a broad variety of allied aircraft, so there are endless possibilities for dissimilar air combat. Each aircraft is fitted with a telemetry pod on one of its Sidewinder launch rails. During air combats off the coast, the pod transmits data to buoys moored at sea and these relay back to base.

After landing, aircrew can replay a computerised recording of their combat on a large screen, allowing them to take in at leisure lessons which might otherwise have been lost in the heat of the fight. To make the most of the range time available, an aircraft which is 'shot down' is merely frozen-out of combat for an agreed time and then permitted to rejoin the fray.

'Decci' provides good weather for most of the year, but those willing to risk the vagaries of the British climate can practise over the similar range in the North Sea. Opened in August 1990 and privately run by British Aerospace, this had attracted 12 customers by late-1994 (many of the foreigners flying from RAF Waddington). Located 80 miles off Lincolnshire, the NSAR can track simultaneously up to 36 aircraft and 50 missile launch simulations, playing back the results to debriefing facilities at Coningsby, Waddington, RNethAFBs Leeuwarden, Twenthe and Volkel and USAFB Lakenheath.

LOW-LEVEL FLYING

Low-level flying is an important part of modern offensive air operations and is routinely practised by RAF aircraft. In the UK, aircraft are restricted to a minimum of 250ft and maximum 450kt (517mph) apart from in three sparsely-populated areas in which the limit is 100ft. Only a small amount of training is conducted in the latter areas, usually in the work-up for squadrons participating in the 'Red Flag' highly realistic combat exercises at Nellis AFB, Nevada, or the similar 'Maple Flag' at CFB Cold Lake. These overseas exercises are valuable training, but the number of European pilots who can participate is necessarily small.

Some of the RAF's low flying is exported to the wastes of Canada, where a detachment of Tornado GR1s is based between April and October under the code name 'Western Vortex'. Crews are flown out to CFB Goose Bay by transport aircraft for short detachments whilst the aircraft, which are donated by several squadrons, remain for the whole season. OLF (Operational Low Flying) is permitted down to 100ft manually or 200ft using the Tornado's automatic terrain-following radar.

In September 1990, Germany imposed a limit of 1,000ft on military aircraft, seriously undermining the RAF's ability to maintain RAFG/No 2 Group at peak efficiency. Consequently, Tornados from Brüggen and Harriers from Laarbruch have made increasing use of UK low flying facilities, although still with diminished training value because of long transit times. From November 1994 onwards, Nos 3/4 Sqn Harriers conducted two-week detachments to the UK to work-up on pilot's night-vision goggles, the German altitude limit preventing realistic training.

BOMBING

Attack aircraft practise bombing both in Canada and the UK, those based in Germany also having their own range at Nordhorn. For reduction of costs, the RAF uses miniature bombs which have the same aerodynamic characteristics as the full-size weapon. The Portsmouth Aviation '3kg' bomb mimics a parachute-retarded 1,000lb bomb

Above left:
'Armour' for the modern knight of the air takes the form of protection against biological and chemical contamination. This Chinook pilot is wearing the AR5 respiration system which includes an airtight head cover with integral visor. The hand-held air-pump (or 'whistling handbag') is discarded when plugged into the aircraft's oxygen system.
Paul Jackson

or the Hunting BL755 cluster bomb, whilst the same firm's '14kg' bomb parallels a 1,000lb 'slick' which may be thrown four miles in a lofting or 'toss-bombing' pull-up type of attack. A flash and smoke cartridge in the bomb is detonated on impact to assist range officers to plot its position. Tornados use the ML Aviation CBLS200 (Carrier, Bomb, Light Stores) practice-bomb carrier, but most other types of aircraft have the older, but similar CBLS100.

Weapons ranges in the UK include Tain and Rosehearty in Scotland; Cowden, Donna Nook, Wainfleet and Holbeach on the east coast; and Luce Bay, where targets are mounted on barges. For practice in use of electronic warfare equipment, aircraft will fly through the training area at Spadeadam, Cumbria, close to which is a dummy airfield on the Otterburn training area, complete with withdrawn aircraft as targets. Live bombing, though rare, takes place on Garvie Island, off the northwest coast of Scotland. Other ranges are used by the MoD for weapons development and at Pembrey by No 4 FTS Hawks for students' advanced training.

When full-size bombs are seen beneath an aircraft, they will usually be blue-painted, concrete-filled practice weapons. Standard RAF bomb is the 1,000lb medium-case high explosive with Mark numbers ranging from 13 to 22. Typical weight with a Hunting Mk 114 'slick' (aerodynamic) tail-fin assembly for lofting attacks is 1,030lb. Retarded by a Hunting Mk 117 parachute tail for low-level delivery, this increases to 1,130lb. Precision delivery is achieved by attaching a Texas Instruments Paveway II laser guidance kit (approximating to the US GBU-10) to

the Mk 13/22 series, increasing total weight to 1,210lb. In July 1994, it was announced that Paveway III (GBU-24) will be ordered as a replacement.

Laser guidance was previously supplied by Buccaneers fitted with the Westinghouse Pave Spike system (known to the USAF as AN/ASQ-153), including the AN/AVQ-23E designator pod on the port inner pylon. The current and more versatile system is GEC-Ferranti's TIALD (Thermal Imaging Airborne Laser Designator) which was first fitted to the port under-fuselage pylon of Tornado GR1s for successful use in the Gulf War — even though it was still in the development stage. No 14 Sqn at Brüggen has been the TIALD Tornado unit since late-1993 (taking over from No 617). Further TIALD pods were ordered in 1994 to equip 12 Jaguar GR1B/T2Bs and more will be needed for Harriers, it was confirmed in July of the same year.

Still in stock are the Mks 1 and 2 bombs of nominal 540lb weight. Free-fall versions weigh 570lb, whilst the Hunting Mk 118 retarding tail increases this to 620lb. Mks 1-2 and 13-22 are fitted with the new Type 960 MFBF

Below:
Bomb away! A retarded 1,000lb bomb falls from an SAOEU Harrier GR7 during a training sortie. The tail parachute, which has just deployed, prevents the weapon from skipping along the ground and missing its target. *Paul Jackson*

(multi-function bomb fuse) which first saw action in the Gulf War of 1991. Hunting also makes cluster-bomb units (CBUs), of which the BL755 (RAF designation L1) is fitted to Jaguars, Harriers and occasionally, Tornado GR1s. It weighs 610lb in original form and 582lb as the Improved BL755. For cratering runways and laying small anti-personnel mines to hamper repair, Tornado GR1s are fitted with two Hunting JP233 bomblet dispensers (RAF type L2) weighing 5,148lb each. The MATRA 155 launcher for 18 68mm SNEB rockets is used occasionally by Harriers and weighs 400lb loaded. For the Gulf War, Jaguars received 530lb Bristol Aerospace (Canada) LAU-5003B/A pods containing 19 CRV-7 high-velocity rockets. These have been retained for potential use in Bosnia.

For the future, Staff Requirement (Air) 1238 is outstanding for an anti-armour missile to replace the free-fall BL755 and SR(A) 1236 covers a conventionally-armed stand-off missile. Eurofighter's medium-range AAM will be chosen under SR(A) 1239, but it has already been decided to fulfil SR(A) 1234 with the BAe ASRAAM as a Sidewinder replacement. Choice of ASRAAM was announced on 3 March 1992 and the first large production order was revealed on 25 May 1994. Still in the conception stage are Air Staff Target 1243 for an autonomously-guided bomb and AST 1246 for an anti-ship missile.

The RAF's nuclear weapon is the WE177 Type B bomb of 100 kilotonnes yield. Weighing 950lb, WE177B is 12ft 0in long and has a tail-fin cross-section of 2ft 0in. In service since September 1966 (with the Vulcan B2), WE177B was due to have been replaced early in the next century by a tactical stand-off missile, for which Staff Requirement (Air) 1244 was issued. This was cancelled on 18 October 1993 when it was decided that some Trident submarine-launched missiles would be modified for tactical nuclear use. WE177B will be withdrawn in around 2005, ending the RAF's nuclear role.

That has already happened with the Nimrod fleet, which was equipped with the WE177A depth charge for national roles and US-supplied B57 equivalents under NATO auspices. In parallel with the withdrawal of nuclear weapons from the Royal Navy's surface vessels and aircraft, Nimrods lost their nuclear tasking in June 1992.

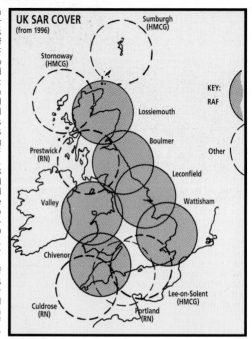

UK SAR COVER (from 1996)

Sumburgh (HMCG)
Stornoway (HMCG)
Lossiemouth
Boulmer
Prestwick (RN)
Leconfield
Valley
Wattisham
Chivenor
Lee-on-Solent (HMCG)
Culdrose (RN)
Portland (RN)

KEY:
RAF
Other

SEARCH AND RESCUE (SAR)

The RAF's 'yellow air force' generates much goodwill for the Service by frequent rescues of civilians in danger, such operations being regarded as training for the primary role of saving downed aircrew. Between 1993 and 1996, the home-based SAR force is undergoing modernisation involving withdrawal of 14 Wessex HC2s and an increase in the Sea King HAR3 fleet from 19 to 25 by the addition of six new Mk 3As. The fleet will then comprise 12 Sea Kings at immediate readiness with six Flights; two in the Falkland Islands; four with the SKOCU at St Mawgan when it upgrades from SKTU in 1996; and seven as an operational and engineering pool. The last-mentioned may also have to provide the planned Sea Kings for No 32 (The Royal) Sqn and No 84 Sqn in Cyprus.

In parallel, some detachments of Nos 22 and 202 Sqn have been moved. The full changes are: Chivenor and Valley upgraded to Sea King; Manston flight transferred to Wattisham; and Brawdy, Coltishall and Leuchars flights withdrawn. Leconfield, Lossiemouth and Boulmer remain unchanged. No 22 Sqn, the Wessex unit, began Sea King conversion on 1 July 1994 when 'A' Flight at Chivenor was re-equipped. Control is now exercised only by the National Rescue

Above:
Amongst the many operations in which the RAF has been involved in the 1990s has been 'Vigour', flying urgently-needed food to Somali refugee camps from a temporary base at Mombasa, Kenya. *Paul Jackson*

Below:
Main photo-reconnaissance assets of the RAF are the Tornados of Nos II (nearest) and 13 Sqn, based at Marham. Canberra PR9s of No 39 (1 PRU) Sqn are generally employed on non-operational tasks such as mapping, but have overflown the Bosnia war zone. Recce pods may also be fitted to Jaguars and Harriers. *Paul Jackson*

Co-ordination Centre at Pitreavie Castle near Edinburgh following mid-1995 decommissioning of its former southern equivalent at Mount Wise, Plymouth.

As shown in the accompanying map, RAF rescue flights are augmented by three provided by the Royal Navy and three by the Coastguard. Additionally, one Puma is kept on SAR stand-by at Aldergrove, Northern Ireland. All RAF helicopters had been modified for use of pilot's night-vision goggles by mid-1993.

BATTLE-DAMAGE REPAIR

As a means of increasing the effective strength of the RAF on the second and subsequent days of a war, techniques have been developed of rapidly repairing damage caused by enemy defences to aircraft in action. The centre of research was the Battle Damage Repair School at Abingdon, although No 431 MU at Brüggen (now disbanded) deserves credit as another pioneer of such work. BDR aims to repair an aircraft in 8-12hr — compared with weeks or months to do the same job with manufacturer's parts. The only rule is that the aircraft must be safe to fly afterwards; within that proviso, ingenious methods are used to patch shell-holes, repair control-rods and splice electrical wiring with any materials to hand.

Combat stations have BDR airframes in the form of aircraft which would otherwise have been scrapped at the end of their operational lives. They serve as subjects for training and for Taceval exercises, when an examiner will declare a squadron aircraft to be unserviceable until a representative repair has been undertaken on the BDR airframe.

TACEVALS

Tacevals (Tactical Evaluations) are part of a NATO assessment procedure for every front-line air base. They come in two parts, the first of which is a no-notice call-out at which squadrons must bring 70% of their aircraft to readiness within 12hr. Part two, some days later, is a broader test of base security and defence, BDR capability, repair of airfield damage (see Territorial Army in the next chapter), medical care, and similar aspects. The international team of examiners awards points in each category and brings any weaknesses to the attention of the station commander.

NATO EXERCISES

Air defence forces have the opportunity to combat simulated raids on the UK during regular exercises, in which other air forces and RAF strike/attack aircraft operating from the Continent play the role of attackers. In 1994, the well-known major events, Elder Forest (held in the spring of even-numbered years) and similar, but smaller, Elder Joust (in the spring and autumn),

were both replaced by new events. Brilliant Invader, the spring (March) exercise was a small-scale affair, but Brilliant Foil (October) was part of the NATO-wide Cold Fire and brought several foreign aircraft to UK air fields to play the part of both 'blue' and 'orange' forces. Also well known, but different in its purpose, the twice-yearly Mallet Blow also brings overseas aircraft to UK to operate alongside the RAF against the Otterburn and Spadeadam weapons ranges.

Below:
**Preparing 30 mm
cannon shells for loading.**

6 RAF Regiment, Reserves and Auxiliaries

Far from all RAF personnel are concerned with the immediate task of getting an aircraft into the air. Others are one step removed from such work, although their activities are no less vital to the efficient and safe operation of every RAF station. This chapter examines the RAF Regiment, Fire Service, Royal Auxiliary Air Force (RAuxAF), RAF Volunteer Reserve (VR) and units of the Army and Territorial Army. In the near future it is intended that the RAuxAF and RAFVR should be combined, although the Air Training Corps and University Air Squadron elements of the VR will not be involved.

ROYAL AUXILIARY AIR FORCE

Having fought with distinction in World War 2, the RAuxAF flying squadrons converted to jet fighters, but disbanded in 1957. Only a small number of ground-based units then remained, including the Maritime HQs, formed as co-ordination centres in November-December 1959 to operate alongside the regular RAF. Numbers were increased from 1979 (when there were just

262 members) onwards with addition of squadrons to the RAF Regiment and with an Air Movements Squadron (formed 1982) in 1982 and Aeromedical Evacuation Squadron in July 1983. Auxiliaries presently number some 1,600.

On 1 April 1986 the RAF began a trial to assess the practicability of placing RAuxAF personnel as aircrew aboard VC10s and Nimrods. This proved to be successful in the case of Nimrod Air Electronics Officers and the RAuxAF was thus able to play a front-line role — albeit small in the 1991 Gulf War, flying with Nos 120 and 201 Sqn. RAuxAF personnel will be shortly added to Nos 15 and 27 Sqn of the RAF Regiment (see below) to assist in manning Rapier SAM installations and it was announced in April 1994 that some would be recruited to fly in Wessex and Hercules.

Current units of this part-time force are listed hereunder. An explanation of RAuxAF Regiment Field Squadron roles will be found under the RAF Regiment heading. Traditionally, squadrons are named for the area from which they draw their volunteers.

● **No 1 Maritime HQ** *'City of Hertford'*	Northwood
● **No 2 Maritime HQ** *'City of Edinburgh'*	Pitrievie Castle
● **No 3 Maritime HQ** *'County of Devon'*	St Mawgan
● **No 4624 'County of Oxford' (Movements) Sqn**	Brize Norton
● **No 4626 'County of Wiltshire' (Aeromedical Evacuation) Sqn**	Lyneham

Royal Auxiliary Air Force Regiment

● No 1310 Wing, HQ; Honington	
● No 2503 'County of Lincoln' Field Sqn	Waddington (No 11 Group)
● No 2620 'County of Norfolk' Field Sqn	Marham (No 1 Group)
● No 2622 'Highlands' Field Sqn	Lossiemouth (No 18 Group)
● No 2624 'County of Oxford' Field Sqn	Brize Norton (No 1 Group)
● No 2625 'County of Cornwall' Field Sqn	St Mawgan (No 1 Group)

On 31 March 1994 three squadrons were disbanded: No 2623 'East Anglian' Field Sqn at Honington; No 2729 'City of Lincoln' at Waddington and No 2890 at Waddington/Coningsby, the two last mentioned having Oerlikon 35mm anti-aircraft cannon. At the same time, No 1339 Wing was also

disbanded, this having administered the Waddington squadrons, Nos 2503 (see above), 2729 and 2890.

Auxiliaries previously provided Defence Flights at Brampton, High Wycombe, Lyneham and St Athan, but it was announced in April 1994 that these were to be disbanded.

RAF VOLUNTEER RESERVE

It is often forgotten that the majority of those who were conscripted into the RAF during World War 2 became members of the RAFVR, not the 'regular' RAF. Now the VR staffs just four Flights,

although there are a further 3,300 unpaid members of the RAFVR (Training) who operate Air Training Corps squadrons and the associated AEFs and VGSs.

● **No 7006 Flight**	High Wycombe	(intelligence)
● **No 7010 Flight**	Wyton	(photographic interpretation)
● **No 7630 Flight**	Ashford	(interrogation)
● **No 7644 Flight**	Uxbridge	(public relations)

ROYAL AIR FORCE REGIMENT

Formed in February 1941 to provide defence of RAF aerodromes, the regiment has a similar role today, using both SAMs and surface transport. The Commandant-General of the Regiment is also responsible for the RAF Police, Security Services and Fire Service, but control of all four is devolved to Commands and stations. All personnel receive initial instruction with the Training Wing of the Regiment Depot, which moved from Catterick to Honington on 1 July 1994 having graduated its final course at the former station on 9 March 1994. The first Honington course was conducted between 30 September 1994 and 1 February 1995.

SHORT RANGE AIR DEFENCE SQUADRONS

SHORAD squadrons are equipped with the British Aerospace Rapier surface-to-air missile and tasked with destroying enemy aircraft attacking aerodromes. No 6 Wing mans Rapiers bought by the US Government for defence of USAF bases in England, but will disband as a consequence of large-scale American withdrawals. For administrative reasons, its squadrons are based on RAF stations in peacetime. All Rapier squadrons spend a month at firing camp on South Uist, Hebrides, each year.

Part of the existing Rapier Field Standard B1 equipment is being replaced by Field Standard C (commercial name, Rapier 2000). Three squadrons and a training unit will be equipped with a total of 26 fire units. These may be easily distinguished from the older units as they have eight mounted rounds instead of four. Misleadingly, Field Standard C was 'rolled out' on 18 January 1995, despite first deliveries having begun in 1993. In fact, No 26 Sqn was first to become operational with Field Standard C, in December 1994, and will be followed by Nos 15, 16 and 37, although the Rapier OEU formed at Honington with FSC on 1 April 1994. In addition, Nos 15 and 27 will be 50% staffed by the RAuxAF Regiment by 1997. The Rapier Mk 2 missile (not to be confused with Field Standards, which refer to the detection, support and launch equipment) was introduced in 1991, going first to No 66 Sqn. First qualification firings were conducted in June 1993.

● No 15 Sqn	Leeming (No 11 Group)
● No 16 (Reserve) Sqn	Honington
	(Depot; OCU)
● No 26 Sqn	Laarbruch
	(RAF Germany)
● No 27 Sqn	Scampton
	(No 11 Group)
● No 37 Sqn	Brüggen (RAF Germany)
● No 48 Sqn	Lossiemouth
	(No 11 Group)
● Rapier OEU	Honington (Depot)
● Resident Squadron	Falkland Islands

Notes:
RAF Germany squadrons were controlled by No 4 Wing at Wildenrath until its disbandment in 1991; the 'old' No 16 Sqn disbanded at Wildenrath in April 1992; No 63 at Gütersloh in October 1992. No 27 reduced to a cadre at Leuchars on 7 February 1995 for transfer to Scampton and will later move to Waddington, although its base remains Leuchars. Numbered squadrons take four-month turns at being the Resident Rapier Squadron on the Falkland Islands.

No 6 Wing, HQ: Honington
● No 19 Sqn	Brize Norton (USAFBs
	Fairford and Upper
	Heyford)
● No 20 Sqn	Honington (USAFBs
	Alconbury, Woodbridge
	and Bentwaters)
● No 66 Sqn	Honington (USAFBs
	Mildenhall and
	Lakenheath)

(HQ No 6 Wing and No 66 Squadron were at West Raynham until May 1994.)

FIELD SQUADRONS

Tracked vehicles have been withdrawn from former Light Armoured Squadrons in 1993-94, reducing them in status to Field Squadrons which have only Land Rovers for mobility. Equipment for air base perimeter defence comprises machine guns and 81mm mortars. RAuxAF Regiment Field Squadrons (2503, etc — see above) are similarly equipped. The Queen's Colour Squadron (formed

Opposite above:
Field Standard C of the BAe Rapier short-range air defence system has an eight-round launcher, replacing the previous four. Three operational squadrons of the RAF Regiment are being equipped.
Paul Jackson

Opposite below:
Defending a field helicopter site against infiltration. Standard-issue armament includes the Light Support Weapon (5.56mm machine gun) (left) and 5.56mm rifle. Paul Jackson

1 November 1960) has ceremonial duties whilst in the UK but is tasked with protection of helicopter units when operating in the field in Germany. No 1 Squadron is similarly involved with defending Harrier sites and No 34 would also transfer to Germany, if required. No 34's last armoured vehicles were withdrawn on 12 August 1994.

● No 1 Field Sqn	Laarbruch
● No 2 Parachute Sqn	Honington
● No 3 Field Sqn	Aldergrove
● No 34 Field Sqn	Akrotiri
● Queen's Colour	
(No 63) Sqn	Uxbridge

Notes:
No 2 Sqn was at Catterick until June 1994. Recent disbandments have included No 51 Sqn at Brüggen on 31 March 1993. QCS was given the number 63 in 1993 after disbandment of the Rapier squadron at Gütersloh. It is the sole regiment squadron in Personnel & Training Command.

Also part of the Regiment is:
● 4001 Training Support Flight Honington

AIR BASE SECURITY

Two forms of base perimeter security are practised. In wartime, the RAF regiment in its vehicles would patrol the area surrounding a combat station whilst all ranks and trades were armed with hand weapons to defend points within the boundary. In peacetime, all stations are patrolled against a terrorist threat. The first sight greeting a visitor arriving at the gate of an RAF installation will often be an L85 (SA80) rifle pointing at them from a slit in a Yarnold Bunker. This is named for Sqn-Ldr Jed Yarnold, RAF Regiment, who devised the system of modifying mains sewer pipes to cheap, but effective miniature pill-boxes, during the mid-1980s reconstruction of Leeming. Similar installations have appeared elsewhere, including a 'double-decker' at Scampton's main gate.

Augmenting basic training at Halton, all new non-commissioned arrivals at an RAF station begin their posting with an average of three days of lectures by the resident Regiment officer and his staff on rifle drill and shooting, first aid, security, basic fire-fighting and other aspects of RAF life. Three or four times per year, airmen up to Flight Sergeant rank have a short refresher course and target practice on the station rifle range before beginning a week of base guarding duties, assisting the RAF police at the gate and making regular rounds of the camp and airfield.

Since 1 April 1984, airwomen have been required to qualify in the use of rifles, but they do not undertake day-to-day guarding duties. (The WRAF was disbanded on 31 March 1994 and its personnel integrated in the RAF.) Previously, personnel of both sexes who were given rifles for wartime use were only half-jokingly referred to as 'cooks and clerks.' With many such trades now sub-contracted to civilian firms, the burden of base security falls on a smaller number of uniformed personnel.

ROYAL AIR FORCE FIRE SERVICE

Administered by the RAF Regiment, the RAFFS also employs locally-based civilians at certain stations. All training is conducted at Manston by the Fire Services Central Training Establishment (formed 1 January 1989 on addition of elements formerly at Catterick). As expected, the FSCTE has a range of instructional airframes — some for burning, some not — but its training aids reflect the fact that it is responsible for all types of fire on RAF stations, including domestic incidents in married quarters. For that reason, a small fire staff must remain on duty even when flying has ceased for the day.

Provision of vehicles is according to the types of aircraft operating from or visiting a station. A typical base would have one Mk 10 Primary 2 fire tender, one Mk 11 Primary 1 and one TACR Mk 2 (Truck, Airfield Crash Rescue) Rapid Intervention Vehicle. Whilst the Mks 10 and 11 resemble civilian fire engines (except for the foam monitor on top), the TACR is a six-wheel Range Rover designed to race to the scene of an aircraft accident. Stations regularly receiving the large TriStar have small turntable ladders added to the Mk 11s, whilst at Mount Pleasant, Falkland Islands, the terrain also demands a Haggelunds BV206 over-snow tracked vehicle towing a rescue trailer.

Below:
RAF firemen are trained at Manston and must be able to deal with all types of fire, not just aircraft. A Mk 11 Primary 1 vehicle is seen during a training exercise. *RAF*

Above opposite:
No 56 (R) Sqn at Coningsby operates its Tornado F3s from a flight-line which has been fitted with multiple fuel hydrants. In place of the large tankers previously used, only a small pump vehicle is required to replenish aircraft. *Paul Jackson*

Below opposite:
The Yarnold Bunker uses commercially-available concrete sewer pipes to produce a cheap, but serviceable, defensive position. *Paul Jackson*

ARMY AND TERRITORIAL ARMY

The Royal Engineers are tasked with assisting RAF Germany to construct forward operating bases and keep permanent stations operational in wartime. In the former category, four squadrons, including one normally based in the UK, would prepare sites for Harriers and Chinooks/Pumas.

A further two home-based squadrons are assigned to airfield damage repair at German bases. Their work would be undertaken in conjunction with RAF personnel trained in disposal of unexploded bombs and aided by two Gazelle HT3s detached from No 2 FTS (painted in camouflage) which would reconnoitre the station after a raid.

● 10 Field Sqn; 48 Field Sqn*	Harrier Force
● 11 Field Sqn; 32 Field Sqn	Helicopter Force
● 50 Field Sqn (Construction)*	Laarbruch
* based in the UK	

On 26 March 1983, No 277 Field Sqn formed as the first Territorial Army (TA) unit dedicated to airfield damage repair. The part-time volunteer units comprise about 84 men, rolls of metal matting to lay over large repaired holes, stocks of quick-drying concrete and a fleet of contractor's plant: typically, three earth-movers, one JCB, six earth-carrying trucks, one excavator, two graders, four general-purpose trucks, four Volvo fork-lift trucks, two Alvis Saracen armoured reconnaissance vehicles, two motor-rollers and three Coles cranes used as compactors. A full-time army Major is in command, and the 27 days per year of training include repair of holes purposely dug into disused sections of taxiway and runway. Units are as above, the full title of each being Field Squadron (Airfield Damage Repair) Royal Engineers (Volunteers).

● 216 Sqn, RE	Marham
● 219 Sqn, RE	Coningsby
● 234 Sqn, RE	Leeming
● 236 Sqn, RE	Kinloss
● 237 Sqn, RE	Lossiemouth
● 267 Sqn, RE	Waddington
● 277 Sqn, RE	Leuchars

(No 212 Sqn disbanded at Wattisham in 1992 and its equipment was transferred to Kinloss to permit formation of No 236 Sqn. In May 1993, No 218 Sqn disbanded at Honington.)

Below:
Even the 'cooks and clerks' have vital war roles. Here, Leeming's personnel train in the recovery of a 'wounded' comrade after a simulated attack on the base. *Paul Jackson*

86

7 Radars for control and defence

Radar is an indispensable aid to the daily operations of aircraft, both at their home base and whilst in transit. When intruding aircraft are being sought, the flying radar station (alias Sentry AEW1) is a vital complement to air defence radars on the ground. In addition to detailing the functions of radar, this chapter presents a brief description of the average aerodrome and its installations.

LOCAL AIR TRAFFIC CONTROL

Before proceeding further, it is as well to redefine terms which have become blurred by misuse. 'Airfield' is a landing area for aircraft. 'Aerodrome' is assumed to be an obsolete name, but that is far from so, as it describes an airfield plus its associated hangars, workshops and accommodation. The aerodrome is also referred to as an 'RAF station' (or USAF base), but this term should include the married quarters and any other related areas belonging to the RAF. Conversely, of course, stations may be devoid of an airfield if their role is radar, storage, administration or communications. Finally, an 'airport' is an aerodrome with customs, immigration, money-changing and other passenger-related facilities. Airports are normally regarded as civilian, but RAF Brize Norton, Lyneham, Brüggen and Akrotiri have most of the services of an airport.

The control tower

In the overall command of the Senior Air Traffic Control Officer (SATCO) — of Squadron Leader or Wing Commander rank — the tower has two separate, but closely connected functions: aerodrome control and radar approach. At all times, the assistant SATCO or a supervising officer will be present and responsible for both operations. Personnel are trained by the Central Air Traffic Control School at Shawbury.

In the glass top to the tower are the Aerodrome Controller (ADC) — ranking between Sergeant and Flight Lieutenant — an assistant and the Duty Aircrew Officer (a member of one of the resident flying units). They control all activity on the airfield (including vehicles); aircraft in the visual circuit (up to 3,000ft and out to five miles) and give clearances for radar approaches.

It is in the darkened Radar Approach Room below that talk-downs are conducted. Here are three Surveillance Radar Controllers, two Talk-down Controllers, an assistant and a switchboard operator. Surveillance radar is usually a Plessey Watchman positioned in one corner of the airfield and used to observe all aircraft within 40 miles, although its maximum range is double that figure. Talk-down controllers use a three-dimensional, twin-screen display provided by the Precision Approach Radar (PAR). The latter looks nothing like a traditional radar, but is a box-shaped construction half-way down the main runway which may be swung a turntable through 180° to view aircraft approaching from either direction.

Not to be forgotten, the Runway Controller — normally a Corporal — has an observation position in a specially designed vehicle parked at the touch-down point (usually on the pilot's left) of the runway in use. Following a change of wind direction, he will drive to the opposite end and plug in to the electricity supplies and land-lines there. The Runway Controller is responsible for activity in his vicinity, including the safety of aircraft taking off and landing. Those taking off are checked to ensure all safety-flags are removed, whilst aircraft on the approach are examined through binoculars — and not just for the obvious omission of failing to lower the undercarriage. Any aircraft entering a dangerous situation will be signalled with a red flare.

Outside the control tower is the airfield identification code and Signals Square. The latter is rarely used, but in former times would convey to pilots by means of symbols what is now transmitted by radio. The two-letter code in white concrete laid into grass is at night repeated in Morse Code by the red Aerodrome Identification Beacon located on a building or unobstructed part of the airfield and by the radio-aid Non-Directional Beacon (if installed). Codes are far from cryptic — such as LM for Lossiemouth and SM for St Mawgan — but are unrelated to the four-letter international aerodrome codes used for flight-planning: EGQS and EGDG respectively, for those cited.

Area controls

Aircraft leaving the aerodrome will often be handed over to a military radar service which will ensure that they are kept a safe distance from other traffic, civil and military. With the closure of Midland Radar at North Luffenham in January 1990 there was a reorganisation of area controls, further extended in April 1994 by closure of Eastern Radar. Control is now exercised over England by the civil/military centre at West Drayton or by Scottish Military Radar at Prestwick. The Civil Aviation Authority's network is used for military control.

At low level, where radar coverage is limited by distance, an advisory service is provided by civil airport and military aerodrome radars which covers nearly the whole of England. Pilots participating in this voluntary Lower Airspace Radar Service contact Surveillance Radar Controllers in individual control towers and are kept clear of known conflicting traffic. A more detailed explanation of procedures will be found in *abc Air Traffic Control*, published by Ian Allan Ltd.

Designated airfields are kept open 24hr per day for emergency use by military or civil aircraft. Known as MEDAs (Military Emergency Diversion Airfields) they are kept staffed and lit throughout the night and constantly monitor the international distress frequencies of 121.5mHz and 243.0mHz. Current MEDAs are Manston (Kent), Leuchars (Fife), St Mawgan (Cornwall) and Brize Norton (Oxfordshire). Additionally, Kinloss, Leeming, Marham, Valley and Waddington remain open until midnight between Monday and Thursday and to 18.00 on Friday to accept emergency landings by hook-equipped tactical aircraft undertaking night flying. In the summer months, Waddington is open to 04.00 to provide cover for Personnel & Training Command training aircraft.

AIRFIELD INSTALLATIONS AND MARKINGS

Most current RAF stations were constructed in the 1930s with permanent buildings and a grass airfield which was upgraded with three concrete runways during World War 2. Arrival of jet aircraft usually implied an increase in length for at least one runway — wherever possible, that facing the prevailing (westerly) wind. V-Bomber bases were designated Class A airfields with even longer, 9,000ft runways. Today, it is rare for a station to

use more than one runway, and the others will probably have been broken up, used for parking or allowed to deteriorate. In wartime, straight stretches of taxiway can act as emergency runways.

Parking areas are connected to the runway by taxiways, which are lit at night with blue lights on both sides. At 225ft from the runway's edge is a compulsory stop line for aircraft and vehicles known as the Holding Position. From there, aircraft receive permission to taxi to the runway by radio; vehicles obey ground-level traffic lights. On a board by the Holding Point, and also painted in large characters on the runway, is the Runway Numbering. Two digits are used, giving the magnetic heading to the nearest ten degrees and omitting the final nought; for example a runway direction between 265 and 274° would be marked '27'. Of course, the magnetic variation is just that — a variation — and its slow movement has caused the redesignation of some runways. Naturally, at the opposite end, the runway is called by another name, the difference always being 18 (in other words, 180°): 08/26, 09/27, 10/28, etc.

Heading towards landing, aircraft will first overfly the approach lighting: white lights on poles of increasing height which are illuminated in poor weather or at night. Like most airfield lighting its intensity can be infinitely controlled. Major runways have directional (headlamp-like) approach lights in the form of a centreline and five cross-bars ('CL5B'); minor ones are two-bar ('CL2B'). The runway threshold is marked with green lights at ground level; the far end with red. Most major runways have side-lighting of two forms: uni-directional and omni-directional. The former is a high intensity white light shining towards the landing aircraft; the latter a low intensity white covered by a glass dome. Minor runways possess only 'omnis'.

Immediately beyond the threshold lights are the Threshold Markings in the form of broad white stripes — inevitably nicknamed 'piano keys' followed by the Runway Numbering. If touching down at the start of the concrete would mean a dangerously low approach over a main road or obstruction, there is a Displaced Threshold some distance along the runway. Broad centreline arrows lead to the marking of a white line crossing the runway and emphasised by four white chevrons.

In the final stages of approach, pilots refer for orientation to two blocks of four lights set slightly back from the threshold to the right and left of the runway. These, the Precision Approach Path Indicators (PAPI), are so aligned that they show

Left:
Final approach to Waddington by a Sentry AEW1 over the 'centreline and five bar' lighting. *Paul Jackson*

white if the aircraft is too high (3.5°, or above) and red if too low (2.5°, or below). When on the optimum 3° glidepath, the pilot sees the inner pair of each block red and the outer pair white. To the ground observer more than a few yards away, they naturally appear red.

In the event of a brake — and, if applicable, braking-parachute — failure, the pilot of a small- or medium-sized aircraft will have one or two safety features in his favour. Tactical aircraft have arrestor hooks which, unlike those of naval aircraft, are spring loaded and cannot be retracted at will. Runways will have two cables stretched across them at least 1,300ft from each end and supported on rubber grommets. These are connected to a Rotary Hydraulic Arrestor Gear (RHAG, or 'rag') set into the ground and operating in the same manner as the systems found on aircraft carriers. Also available — perhaps when a taxiway is being used for landing — is the G+W 'Portarrest' Portable Arrestor Gear (PAG) mounted on a pair of wheeled trailers firmly secured to the ground. Boards by the side of the runway mark the RHAG and others, along its whole length, display a single number counting-down the thousands of feet to the runway's end.

The back-up for RHAG/PAG is the arrestor barrier at the extreme end of the runway. Generally, this is a Befab Mk 12A or 12B, the designation abbreviated to RAF A or RAF B. Made of elastic material, the barrier will stop a slow moving fighter with little damage, but it is lowered when there is a take-off or a large aircraft is landing — it being of little help to a TriStar, for example.

AIR DEFENCE RADARS

Assisted by the Sentry AEW1, ground radar stations and control centres are responsible for the air defence of the United Kingdom and its coastal waters. By agreement with NATO, the RAF covers most of NATO Early Warning Area 12, its 'beat' being known as the UK Air Defence Region (UKADR). Covering 750,000sq miles and stretching 1,100 miles from north to south, the UKADR includes all of UK land, plus most of the airspace between southern Norway and Iceland. It is divided into two parts, of which Sector 1 is the airspace north of 55° N (ie, Newcastle-upon-Tyne), and Sector 2, the remainder. Tornado F3s on QRA stand ready to investigate aircraft transiting the ADR which have not filed a flight-plan.

Main control centres are underground, principal of which is the Air Defence Operations Centre at Strike Command HQ, High Wycombe; its reserve is the Secondary ADOC at Bentley Priory, Stanmore — the home of No 11 Group. Sectors 1 and 2 each have a Sector Operations Centre (SOC) and a secondary (which is also a Control & Reporting Centre — CRC), all four equipped with an R3 underground bunker, although the southernmost (Ash) is

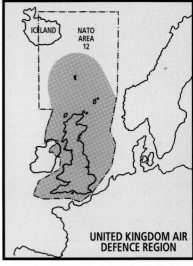

UNITED KINGDOM AIR DEFENCE REGION

non-operational. At the lowest level in the hierarchy are Control & Reporting Points (CRP), all above ground. It is interesting to note that the CRP on the Faroe Islands is entirely controlled and operated by Denmark despite being part of the UKADR. All Fighter Controllers are trained by the School of Fighter Control, Boulmer, and some may be posted to No 8 Sqn to fly in the Sentry AEW1, duly wearing an aircrew half-wing brevet marked 'FC'.

The world of air defence radars has changed dramatically during the past few years. In 1977, the RAF began a '10-year' improvement programme for No 11 Group's assets, although some aspects have taken longer to come on line. In addition to refurbishment of underground CRCs, radars have been replaced and a new computerised communications network installed. The latter, Improved UK Air Defence Ground Environment/Improved Communications & Control System (I-UKADGE/ICCS) was delayed by software problems, but now provides rapid transfer of data between all radar control sites, allowing one to take over the functions of any other which is incapacitated.

As a result of this centralisation of control, above-ground sites no longer are required to communicate directly with aircraft. The final station to be tied into I-UKADGE was Saxa Vord, which controlled its last interception (a staged affair flown by the AOC No 11 Group) on 2 September 1993. Saxa's controlling is now performed at Buchan where the R3 bunker achieved limited IOC in September 1992. Buchan's southern counterpart, Neatishead, became operational in the R3 on 19 April 1993, allowing I-UKADGE to be declared fully functional officially on 1 June 1993. Immediately afterwards,

AIR DEFENCE RADARS

Boulmer (the secondary to Buchan) began transfer to its R3. All the R3s are, in fact, old 'holes' abandoned after the 1957 defence White Paper scaled down the air defence force. First to be refurbished was Ash which, as noted above, has not been commissioned. Instead, it has been the training centre (OCU) for I-UKADGE operators and officially became the Ground Environment Operational Evaluation Unit on 1 October 1993. I-UKADGE has allowed the Strike Command Mobile Radar Reserve at Ty Croes in Anglesey to be tied into the air defence network.

Also delayed is JTIDS (Joint Tactical Information Distribution System, otherwise known as NATO Link 16), which is a secure net operating between ground stations, ships and aircraft, intended to be part of I-UKADGE. The Sentry AEW1 has interim JTIDS capability using the existing Link 11, but terminals have only recently been installed in Tornado F3s of the Operational Evaluation Unit. The first realistic trial was on 27 October 1993 when two Tornados, a Sentry and its French E-3F SDA equivalent conducted an airborne exchange of messages and communicated with ground stations. In July 1994, Tornado F3s from ADOEU and No 5 Sqn conducted further interoperability trials with the USAF at Mountain Home AFB. Nos 5 and 29 Squadrons at Coningsby will be the first with JTIDS, but their aircraft are then destined for Leuchars.

The third major aspect of aid defence modernisation has been replacement of the large, static (and thus vulnerable to air attack) 80-series radars built in the 1960s. The three core stations were then Boulmer, Staxton Wold and Neatishead, each with a Type 84 and Type 85. Buchan's main was a Type 80, in common with many other East Coast stations, long since closed, but Benbecula had the unique Type 88 obtained from the Army. The last-mentioned was first to be decommissioned, in the spring of 1988. Boulmer's Type 85 was the last of its class when closed down in October 1991, whilst Buchan switched off the Type 80 for the last time on 7 April 1993. The final 80-series radar in the UK is the Type 84 at Neatishead which was officially stood-down on

19 July 1993. However, because of problems with the replacement Type 93s, the old T84 continued to be run-up once per month at least until the beginning of 1995. (Another Type 84 remains on Mount Olympus, Cyprus.)

The new air defence radars are mainly Types 91, 92 and 93, which have been augmented by others obtained for specific locations. T91-93 are intended to be mobile to improve security from air attack and are often located away from their home base. For example, Neatishead's T91 is at Trimingham and its T93 at Hopton — both coastal sites. Training exercises involve radars being dismantled and transferred to alternative sites, as would be the case in wartime. Current and recent RAF air defence radars are listed below:

- **Type 90** Marconi S713A Martello; one for trials at Boulmer; withdrawn.
- **Type 91** Marconi S723 Martello; four delivered from 1987, plus one on Faroe Islands.
- **Type 92** General Electric TPS-592; two delivered from 1984.
- **Type 93** Plessey-ITT AR 320; six delivered 1988-89, but not formally accepted by early-1995.
- **Type 94** Plessey AR-3D; two in Falkland Islands.
- **Type 95** Marconi S259; one for mobile reserve.
- **Type 96** Marconi S649; one delivered 1979.
- **Type 97** Marconi S600; two in Falkland Islands.
- **Type 99** Westinghouse TPS-43; one captured from Argentina in 1982.
- **Type 101** Siemens-Plessey AR327; three ordered in January 1994 for delivery from late-1995.

Below:
One of the nine controllers' positions aboard a Sentry AEW1. RAF Sentries have participated in the Deny Flight operations over Bosnia, flying over the Adriatic or in Hungarian airspace.
Paul Jackson

Radars are operated as separate mobile installations by numbered Signals Units. The current disposition is given below, many CRCs and CRPs having two assigned radars.

Location/role	Type	Operator
Sector 1 (Buchan)		
● Faroe Islands CRP	S723	Denmark
● Saxa Vord CRP	Type 93	No 91 SU
	Type 96	
● Buchan SOC/CRC	Type 92	No 487 SU
	Type 93	No 170 SU
● Benbecula CRP	Type 92	No 71 SU
● Boulmer CRC (& reserve SOC)	Type 91	No 75 SU
	Type 93	No 500 SU
Sector 2 (Neatishead)		
● Staxton Wold CRP	Type 91	No 129 SU
	Type 93	No 146 SU
● Ty Croes CRP	Type 93	No 144 SU
● Neatishead SOC/CRC	Type 91	No 432 SU
	Type 93	No 86 SU
● Ash (OEU)	nil	
● Portreath CRP	Type 91	No 405 SU
Overseas — Falkland Islands		
● Byron Heights	Type 94	No 7 SU
● Mt Alice	Type 94	No 751 SU
● Mt Kent	Type 97	No 303 SU
● Pleasant Peak	Type 97	
Overseas — Cyprus		
● Mt Olympus	Type 84	

Additionally supplying data to the UKADR is the Ballistic Missile Early Warning System installation at Fylingdales, North Yorkshire. Here, the famous three 'golfballs', each covering an AN/FPS-49 radar, were decommissioned on 1 October 1992 when the single, three-faced AN/FPS-115 was declared operational. Although paid for by the USA, Flyingdales is operated entirely by the RAF as a partner to two other stations at Clear (Alaska) and Thule (Greenland). With missile attack less likely, the station is mainly occupied with tracking the 7,200 or so satellites and items of 'space junk' currently orbiting the earth.

Opposite:
The AN/FPS-115 radar at Fylingdales is 119ft high and has three faces, only one of which can be seen in this view. Beams are steered electronically, so there is no need for mechanical rotation and the system can track 800 objects simultaneously, compared with 12 per minute with the old AN/FPS-49 system. Redundant 'golfballs' were dismantled in 1994. *Paul Jackson*

Below:
Local control is the 'glasshouse' atop the control tower, in this case Mount Pleasant, Falkland Islands. *RAF*

Now absent from the order of battle is the Royal Observer Corps. A direct-reporting element of Strike Command, the Corps was a valuable aircraft-monitoring asset in World War 2, which later added to its duties the plotting of nuclear fallout. Nearly all its posts were all stood-down during the second half of 1991, immediately following the withdrawal of the 90% of its funding provided by the Home Office. However, a small element concerned with fallout monitoring was retained.

It is convenient to mention here for completeness the other known RAF Signals Units. All are believed to be concerned with communications, such as No 1001 which is the main satellite terminal for the Skynet 4 system, augmented by terminals at Defford and Colerne.

- No 1 SU   Rudloe Manor
- No 2 SU   Bampton Castle
- No 9 SU   Boddington
- No 12 SU   Episkopi, Cyprus
- No 33 SU   Ayios Nikolaos, Cyprus
- No 81 SU   Bampton Castle
- No 280 SU Akrotiri, Cyprus
- No 399 SU Digby
- No 591 SU Digby
- No 840 SU Lindholme
- No 1001 SU Oakhanger

(Recent disbandments are No 6 SU at Rudloe Manor on 14 October 1994, having been supplanted by No 1 SU; and No 26 SU at Gatow, Berlin, on 30 November 1994.)

8 Names, ranks and numbers

The technological world is largely covered by oceans of acronyms and jargon. A brief, two-part guide to these appears below, its second section capturing some of the slang to be heard on the average RAF station. Ranks are hard for the layman to decypher, and so a short course of instruction into their mysteries is herewith appended. Finally, numbers, in the form of an explanation of aircraft accident or repair categories and servicing procedures.

ABBREVIATIONS AND ACRONYMS

A&AEE	Aircraft & Armament Evaluation Establishment (Aeroplane & A Experimental E up to 31 March 1992)
AAM	Air-to-Air Missile
AAR	Air-to-Air refuelling
ACCGS	Air Cadets' Central Gliding School
ADIZ	Air Defence Identification Zone
ADOEU	Air Defence Operational Evaluation Unit (see F3OEU)
AEF	Air Experience Flight
AOC(-in-C)	Air Officer Commanding(-in Chief)
ATC (1)	Air Traffic Control
ATC (2)	Air Training Corps
Attack	Offensive action with conventional weapons (cf Strike)
BBMF	Battle of Britain Memorial Flight
CATCS	Central Air Traffic Control School
CFS	Central Flying School
COC	Combat Operations Centre
CRC	Control and Reporting Centre
CRP	Control and Reporting Post
DERA	Defence Evaluation & Research Agency
DRA	Defence Research Agency
DT&EO	Defence Test & Evaluation Organisation
ECM	Electronic Countermeasures
ELINT	Electronic Intelligence (gathering)
EOD	Explosive Ordnance Disposal
ESM	Electronic Support Measures
ETPS	Empire Test Pilots' School
F3OEU	Tornado F3 Operational Evaluation Unit
FTS	Flying Training School
HAS	Hardened Aircraft Shelter
I-UKADGE	Improved UKADGE (qv)
JEFTS	Joint Elementary Flying Training School
OCU	Operational Conversion Unit
Paveway	Laser guided bomb
PRU	Photographic Reconnaissance Unit
QRA(I)	Quick Reaction Alert (Interceptor)
RAuxAF	Royal Auxiliary Air Force
RIC	Reconnaissance Intelligence Centre
RRS	Regional Reinforcement Squadron
SAOEU	Strike/Attack Operational Evaluation Unit
SATCO	Senior Air Traffic Control Officer
SARTU	Search And Rescue Training Unit
SKTU	Sea King Training Unit
SOC (1)	Sector Operations Centre
SOC (2)	Struck Off Charge
Strike	Offensive action with nuclear weapons (cf Attack)
SSR (1)	Secondary Surveillance Radar
SSR (2)	SACEUR's Strategic Reserve
TQF	The Queen's Flight (part of No 32 Sqn from 1 April 1995)
TTTE	Trinational Tornado Training Establishment
TWCU	Tornado Weapons Conversion Unit
UKADR	United Kingdom Air Defence Region
UKADGE	United Kingdom Air Defence Ground Environment
UAS	University Air Squadron
VASS	Visiting Aircraft Servicing Squadron
VGS	Volunteer Gliding School

RAF-SPEAK

Bimble	Meander, wander (replaces 'stooge')
Bimble Box	Packed lunch
Bluey	Airmail letter form
Bone Dome	Flying helmet
Boss	Squadron commander
Bunny Suit	Aircrew's thermal underclothing
Chippie	De Havilland Chipmunk T10
Christmas Tree	Aircraft robbed of parts to service others
F3	Panavia Tornado F3
Fat Albert	Lockheed C-130K Hercules C1/C3
Gozome	Anything concerning the end of an overseas tour
GR1	Panavia Tornado GR1
GR7	BAe Harrier GR7
Green Writing	Information on a computer display screen or HUD
Groupie	Group Captain
Hangar Queen	Notoriously and regularly unserviceable aircraft
Hindenburgers	Tornado F3's 495gall drop-tanks
Hot to trot	Ready to go
Kit	Almost any piece of equipment or apparatus
Low-Viz	Low visibility paint scheme for aircraft
Meccano	Shorts S312 Tucano T1

MoD Plod	Ministry of Defence Policeman
Noddy Suit	NBC protection clothing
Prod	Engagement of an in-flight refuelling drogue
Rag	Runway arrestor gear
Shadow Squadron	
	Reserve Squadron wartime identity of an OCU
Slurp	Refuelling
Stash	Station Commander (pronounced 'stay-shh")
Talking Freight	Navigator (in pilot-speak)
Timmy	Lockheed TriStar C2/C2A
Tits-up	Unserviceable
Tommy	Lockheed TriStar KC1
Up To Speed	Functioning correctly
Walter	Westland Wessex HC2
Whistling Handbag	
	Hand-held electric ventilator for AR5 respirator
Winder	AIM-9 Sidewinder AAM
Wokka	Boeing Helicopters Chinook HC2 (absorbed from Army-speak)
Zap	Unauthorised unit badge application on a visiting aircraft

RANKS

Two separate career streams are open to those joining the RAF: non-commissioned or commissioned.

Non-commissioned

Rank	Arm badge
● Aircraftman	nil
● Leading Aircraftman	Two-bladed propeller
● Senior Aircraftman	Three-bladed propeller
● Junior Technician	Four-bladed propeller
● Corporal	Two chevrons
● Sergeant	Three chevrons
● Chief Technician	Three chevrons and four-bladed propeller
● Flight Sergeant	Three chevrons and crown
● Warrant Officer	The Royal Arms

Notes:
Aircraftwoman where appropriate. Sergeant, Flight Sergeant and Warrant Officer aircrew add the RAF eagle above their chevrons or below the Royal Arms. (The debate surfaces within the RAF every few years of whether its badge depicts an eagle or an albatross. The insignia, authorised on 15 September 1949 is officially described: 'In front of a circle inscribed with the motto "Per Ardua Ad Astra" and ensigned with the Imperial Crown, an eagle volant and affrontee, head lowered and to the sinister'.)

Commissioned

Rank	Insignia
● Pilot Officer	Thin band
● Flying Officer	Medium band
● Flight Lieutenant	Two medium bands

● Squadron Leader	Medium, thin, medium bands
● Wing Commander	Three medium bands
● Group Captain	Four medium bands
● Air Commodore	One thick band
● Air Vice Marshal	One thick, one medium band
● Air Marshal	One thick, two medium band
● Air Chief Marshal	One thick, three medium bands
● Marshal of the RAF	One thick, four medium bands

Note:
All bands are dark blue with a light blue centre. Thin 1/4in; medium 9/16in; thick 1 3/4in.

Cadet and probationary ranks not included, although university students will fly BAe Bulldogs in the rank of Acting Pilot Officer.

Qualification badges
Within certain limits, trade and qualification badges are worn irrespective of rank. Ground trades such as telecommunications, PT Instructor and musician have their own badge, as do voluntary qualifications including marksman and member of a mountain rescue team. Air Steward and Flight Nursing Attendant have two-winged *arm* badges. Aircrew qualifications are worn on the left chest in the form of a pair of wings for pilots and a single wing for other airborne qualifications.

The single-wing design includes an appropriate letter or symbol, those in current use being AE — Air Electronics, AT — Airborne Technician, E — Engineer, FC — Fighter Controller, LM — Air Loadmaster, N — Navigator, S — Air Signaller and (parachute symbol) — Parachute Jumping Instructor. These badges may be worn when the qualification has expired through lack of practice and in extremely rare cases individuals can wear two half-wings following a change of career. Medal ribbons (if any) are worn below the wings and can include campaign awards (Cyprus, South Atlantic 1982, etc) and civil honours (OBE, MBE, etc) as well as decorations for airborne service and gallantry.

INCIDENT AND ACCIDENT CATEGORIES

Since 1952, the RAF has used a numbering system for classifying aircraft unserviceability states and indicating, approximately, the degree of effort required to return them to the air. It is popularly supposed that when an aircraft is issued with a Category number that it has been involved in an accident; in fact, aircraft are also thus classified when out of service for overhaul or modification.

Classifications and their meanings are:
● Category 1   Undamaged or unaffected

- ● Category 2   Rectification possible with resources of the operating unit
- ● Category 3   Requires attention of specialist RAF unit, as beyond the resources of operating unit
- ● Category 4   Cannot be repaired on site; requires transportation to the manufacturer's premises
- ● Category 5   Struck off charge as:
  - Cat 5C   reduced to components
  - Cat 5FA   flying accident
  - Cat 5GA   ground accident
  - Cat 5GI   ground instruction airframe
  - Cat 5M   missing
  - Cat 5S   scrap

SERVICING INTERVALS

Most aircraft servicing is based on hours flown, rather as that for a car is determined by mileage. The majority of this work can be accomplished at station level, either by the squadron or the base engineering wing, but 'Majors' are normally undertaken at St Athan or by the contractor. The interval between 'Majors' determines the frequency of other work, and on entry of an aircraft into service is set at an arbitrary level. As experience builds, that can be extended, a case in point being the Tornado GR1 which began with 1,200hr and has been raised to 1,600hr and now 2,000hr.

The 2,000hr cycle involves some form of inspection and work every 125hr — in other words, 16 servicings, including the Major. In escalating order of comprehensiveness, these are Primary, Primary Star, Minor, Minor Star and Major, the chronological sequence of which is given below.

Servicing	Hours
Primary	125
Primary Star	250
Primary	375
Minor	500
Primary	625
Primary Star	750
Primary	875
Minor Star	1,000
Primary	1,125
Primary Star	1,250
Primary	1,375
Minor	1,500
Primary	1,625
Primary Star	1,750
Primary	1,875
Major	2,000

Servicing intervals are different in the case of civil airliners such as the RAF's TriStars. These are overhauled on a calendar basis with an hours 'back-stop' which is only reached with — what is for military operations, but not civil — unusually high utilisation. TriStar data is: Primary, three months or 450hr; Primary Star, six months/950hr; Primary Two Star 12 months/1,800hr; Minor, 24 months/3,600hr; and major, 48 months/7,200hr. For a combat aircraft, 7,200hr would represent a respectable lifetime of 20 years.

Many of the Canberras recently withdrawn from service had flown 6,000-9,000hr since the early-1950s, the record perhaps being held by WF916 which retired in 1994 with 10,635. Even Jet Provost T3A XN589 only accumulated 8,878hr of 'circuit-bashing' between June 1961 and 3 March 1993, when it was retired. Very few of the last Lightnings in service had passed 4,000hr, but when the RAF bought its secondhand VC10s for K2/K3 tanker conversion they each had some 45,000hr 'on the clock.'

After its Major overhaul, the aircraft returns to the beginning of the cycle, which may be repeated several times during its lifetime. With regular replacement of parts, an aircraft can be made to last for ever, but in practice it begins its flying career with a life reckoned in fatigue points. The expected life is termed 100 Fatigue Index and after each sortie engineers keep tally of the stresses to which a machine has been subjected — helped by on-board counting equipment in the most modern. Some machines will be withdrawn before reaching 100 and some after; the 100 points is purely an arbitrary number beyond which it is expected that maintenance of the aircraft will become disproportionately costly.

Interestingly, because they were required for important work, aircraft in the Victor K2 fleet had their expected lives extended by 27% to 127 FI and some were cleared after minor structural modifications to 132 FI. It is important to understand that hours do not equate directly to FI, as the latter is determined by the nature of the sorties undertaken. Victor tankers which had been previously B2(SR)s cruising on high-altitude reconnaissance sorties suffered less fatigue than B2s practising low-level penetration in the turbulent lower air. When Victors were retired in October 1993, the highest-houred aircraft was XM717 (the youngest) with 8,250, but 126.8 FI. Conversely, the most fatigued was XL190 with 130.15 FI, despite only 5,370hr.